LYNN CRAWFORD'S
PITCHIN' IN

LYNN CRAWFORD'S
PITCHIN' IN

GREAT RECIPES FROM THE ULTIMATE ROAD TRIP, AND MORE

LYNN CRAWFORD

PENGUIN
an imprint of Penguin Canada

Published by the Penguin Group
Penguin Group (Canada), 90 Eglinton Avenue East, Suite 700, Toronto, Ontario, Canada M4P 2Y3

Penguin Group (USA) Inc., 375 Hudson Street, New York, New York 10014, U.S.A.
Penguin Books Ltd, 80 Strand, London WC2R 0RL, England
Penguin Ireland, 25 St Stephen's Green, Dublin 2, Ireland (a division of Penguin Books Ltd)
Penguin Group (Australia), 707 Collins Street, Melbourne, Victoria 3008, Australia
(a division of Pearson Australia Group Pty Ltd)
Penguin Books India Pvt Ltd, 11 Community Centre, Panchsheel Park, New Delhi – 110 017, India
Penguin Group (NZ), 67 Apollo Drive, Rosedale, Auckland 0632, New Zealand (a division of Pearson New Zealand Ltd)
Penguin Books (South Africa) (Pty) Ltd, 24 Sturdee Avenue, Rosebank, Johannesburg 2196, South Africa

Penguin Books Ltd, Registered Offices: 80 Strand, London WC2R 0RL, England

First published in Viking hardcover by Penguin Canada, 2012

Published in this edition, 2012

1 2 3 4 5 6 7 8 9 10 (WEB)

Food Photography: Kathleen Finlay
Prop and Food Stylist: Sasha Seymour
Food Stylist and Recipe Tester: Lora Kirk
Additional Photography: Frantic Films Corporation, Kuba Psuty

The book is based on the television series *Pitchin' In*, which is produced by Frantic Films Corporation
and broadcast in Canada by Food Network Canada. The publisher acknowledges
Frantic Films Corporation's participation in respect to elements from the show featured in the book.

Manufactured in Canada.

Library and Archives Canada Cataloguing in Publication

Crawford, Lynn
Pitchin' in / Lynn Crawford.

Includes index.
ISBN 978-0-14-318112-5

1. Cooking. 2. Cookbooks. 3. Pitchin' in (Television program). I. Title.

TX715.C684 2012   641.5   C2012-906117-4

Visit the Penguin Canada website at **www.penguin.ca**

Special and corporate bulk purchase rates available;
please see **www.penguin.ca/corporatesales** or call 1-800-810-3104, ext. 2477.

I dedicate this book to all the farmers, growers, fishermen, and ranchers I have met on this incredible journey. I thank you all for your generous hospitality, heart, passion, commitment, and inspiration.

CONTENTS

INTRODUCTION

My life has changed in so many ways over the past few years. I am a cook; I always have been. I could not think of anything else I'd rather do. I would be lost if I could not slice, chop, whisk, peel, and cook something each and every day. I have always been driven to create a perfect dish, a perfect meal ... each day to work harder and to cook better.

I'm always on fire with ideas. I have an active imagination that means that if I think it, I want to do it. Plans, hopes, dreams: my mind is always busy with a million thoughts. It was really just two simple thoughts that led me to set out on my *Pitchin' In* adventure and to create this cookbook.

Connections are everything. That was my first thought. I don't mean who you know, as in celebrities or power hitters, but who you know on a pure human level. The root of understanding and knowledge comes from being connected. Who do you know?

And the second thought was that I love to cook. The higher I climbed the culinary ladder, the farther away from the food I got. I was the Executive Chef of a luxury hotel in New York City. I was on top of the mountain. I loved living in the Big Apple. I worked with an amazingly talented and committed team. I could pick up the phone and, almost magically, any ingredient I wanted—lobsters, truffles, the best quality beef, fish, seafood, or caviar—would appear instantly. You name it, I got it, without any effort on my part. I loved my job and the people I worked with, but there was only one problem: I was not cooking anymore and I knew that I needed to change my direction. It was one of the hardest decisions I have ever made, but I left my 24-year career with the Four Seasons. It was with a real longing for understanding, and a need to reconnect, that I embarked on my adventurous, hands-on "apprenticeship" in the farming trenches of North America with *Pitchin' In*.

Whether you are trying to connect to a person, place, thing, or idea, you have to experience it directly. You have to "walk a mile in their shoes," so they say, and only then can you understand the what, why, and how of something. For me, the two connections I wanted most were with people and food. And I didn't want those connections to be exclusive—meet some people and find some food—I wanted it to be inclusive. My goal was to meet the people who produce the food so that I could understand everything that went into making that product the best in its domain.

If you've seen *Pitchin' In*, you know I don't shy away from dirty jobs and hard work. I never thought I could get that dirty, stinky, sweaty, cold, hot, wet, parched, embarrassed, humiliated, nauseated, or grossed out. I used to think working in a kitchen was tough work. Have I ever learned a thing or two—the hard way. Try hauling thousands of pounds of mussels out of the cold waters off the coast of Prince

Edward Island on a blustery cold day in April. Or, in Alberta, how about corralling an angry two-thousand-pound wild bison into a tiny space to vaccinate her. What about battling the heat, humidity, and insects as you're dragging around a swamp loading and unloading crawfish traps in Louisiana.

I have a much finer appreciation for cream since visiting a dairy farm and assisting a vet with a pregnancy test. Or turkey: how can a frozen ball of protein and fat wrapped in a tight white plastic bag compare to a free-range, native North American bird that I have personally chased through a field while trying to keep my pants from falling down (without luck). The chasing, the feeding, and the cleaning have richly added to my understanding of these foods, and that understanding has given me the knowledge I need to create better dishes and be a better chef.

That's how it all comes full circle. Because through the food I prepare and serve, I also want to connect with people, whether it's friends and family, or guests at my restaurant. To my mind nothing is as intimate or visceral as the gift of food prepared with passion and thought. It touches all the senses, while evoking a warmth and connection for both the giver and the receiver. So, when a fisherman who has worked for days catching pink shrimp the best way he can gives me some of his shrimp, I understand and feel the pride and love that went into fishing his product. Then when I prepare those shrimp to the best of my ability for my dinner guests, I pass that feeling along with the love that I embedded in the dish. The diner enjoys all this "back story" combined with delicious, fresh taste. It's all connected.

And now you're connected. I hope reading this book will inspire you to explore, get to know where your food comes from, and be hands-on with your food. I encourage you to meet the producers at your local farmers' market and get out to some u-picks in the country.

Get dirty if you have to. These valuable experiences will make you a better cook, and you'll be giving back to the hard-working farmers, growers, and fishermen who give us these amazing products. It's about appreciation—on both sides.

I found this out starting with my very first *Pitchin' In* adventure and it has been true in every case since then. The farmer often doesn't get to see what happens down the line with his product. And you know, after all the care they take, and the hardships, don't think they don't wonder where that peach or that shrimp will end up. In every episode of the show, I get to cook for the rancher or farmer or fisherman I worked with, and I never fail to see their pride in the great products they've produced. It's always a special moment and it makes each journey complete. I hope when you meet a farmer at the market, or at a roadside stand, you get the chance to talk with them about what you're thinking of creating with their product. No doubt they'll be pleased to tell you their story about how they grew the food and a connection will be made. It'll inspire ideas.

Inspiration comes from everything. On my *Pitchin' In* adventure, I've been dazzled by the Booyah recipe of a 100-year-old Minnesotan, tried the most incredible avocados fresh off the tree, swooned at the awesome beauty (if that's the word) of a Dungeness crab pulled from the cold waters of the Pacific Ocean, and marvelled at a microwaved lobster on a Nova Scotia dock. All of these experiences have inspired the recipes that are here in this book. I hope you get a sense of not only the food but also the history, the muscle, and the true grit behind the food, and the feeling that went into it. It's a rich process that brings a meal to the table.

I now know first-hand that farming and fishing are hard physical work. It's what I signed up for. It is what I wanted to do. The people

I have met on this journey have completely changed my life. They have given me the biggest gift anyone could give a chef. I have been allowed to experience just a taste of what they do each and every day. I know that I will never take any ingredient for granted again. These experiences have changed how I cook and how I look at food because I now know what it takes to produce it and the people who are committed to producing the best quality without compromise.

What an amazing adventure this has been. Hands down, the opportunity of a lifetime! I have never been happier. I love cooking today more than I ever have, and I do know one thing for sure—it's best that I stay in the kitchen and leave the farming and fishing for those with the talent!

The recipes in this book were created by using the most incredible ingredients that I have had the privilege to harvest from the fields, forests, and waters and cook with. These recipes are all inspired by those people I met along the way. Connecting through beautiful food is the ultimate pleasure for me. Now, when I prepare a meal and sit down to share it with a table of friends, moments stretch and become memorable. All my personal favourite things happen: camaraderie, laughter, pride, respect, and stories—new and newly embellished. All of a sudden, everything has a place. Being inspired, connected, and staying present in the moment is what makes for an amazing food adventure. Come on, what's better than that? I wish that for you through this book and through your own marvels and adventures ... and just remember to never stop cooking with heart.

Chef Lynn

ON THE BOAT

MUSSELS

The ocean, with its magical, mysterious alchemy, has sustained us since the beginning of time. Prince Edward Island is one of the best places in the world to grow and harvest shellfish of pretty much any kind, including beautiful mussels and clams.

There is nothing like a fresh mussel you muscle out of the water and put straight into your mouth. With seafood especially, fresh is best. But really it's my mantra for any ingredient. Why not, when we have amazing local producers across the country whose passion for their product is in the very taste of it? As soon as I tasted P.E.I. mussels, I was inspired with ideas. That's the thing about a great ingredient and knowing first-hand where it came from—the ordinary is already extraordinary and the exotic is divine. The rich, sweet flavour and firm texture of P.E.I. mussels can handle basically anything you throw at them, like cooking them on lemongrass skewers and serving them with a spicy curry, which pretty much blew the minds of the fishermen I was with.

Every time I get the chance to eat something right out of the sea, or for that matter fresh off the branch or straight from the field, it inspires me and gets my own mojo going. And that back and forth between the food and the chef is what I love and what makes for amazing culinary adventures.

TIPSY MUSSELS WITH SMOKY BACON

Mussels cultured in the cool waters surrounding P.E.I. are sweet, tender, and plump. One of my favourite ways to eat mussels is to steam them in beer with lots of bacon. Adding a touch of cream and mustard makes an amazing, creamy, rich, smoky broth.

Serves 4

4 slices smoked bacon, cut into ½-inch (1 cm) pieces
1 tbsp (15 mL) unsalted butter
2 stalks celery, diced
2 leeks (white and pale green parts only), thinly sliced
4 cloves garlic, sliced
2 sprigs thyme
1 bottle (12 oz/341 mL) wheat beer
2 tbsp (30 mL) whole grain mustard
½ cup (125 mL) heavy cream
Salt and pepper
4 lb (2 kg) mussels, scrubbed and debearded
¼ cup (60 mL) chopped parsley

In a large pot over medium heat, cook the bacon until crispy. Remove with a slotted spoon and set aside. Add the butter to the bacon fat. When it has melted, add the celery, leeks, garlic, and thyme. Cook, stirring frequently, until the vegetables are soft. Turn the heat up and deglaze the pan with the beer. When the liquid is reduced by half, stir in the mustard, cream, and salt and pepper; bring to a boil. Add the mussels, stir once, and cover. Cook until the mussels just begin to open, about 5 minutes. Remove the lid, stir the mussels (discard any that haven't opened), and garnish with the bacon and parsley.

3 tbsp (50 mL) finely diced red onion

2 tbsp (30 mL) lime juice

1 avocado, peeled and diced

2 lobsters, cooked and shelled (page 23), chilled, and diced, claws reserved for garnish

3 tbsp (50 mL) chopped cilantro

Salt and pepper

1 romaine heart, finely shredded, plus 4 small leaves reserved for garnish

Cocktail Sauce (page 255) or Lemon Rémoulade (page 252)

4 lemon wedges

In a medium bowl, combine the onion and lime juice. Let stand for a few minutes. Add the avocado, lobster meat, and cilantro. Combine well and season with salt and pepper.

Divide the shredded romaine lettuce evenly among 4 martini glasses or salad plates. Spoon the lobster avocado salad onto the lettuce. Top each serving with 1 tbsp (15 mL) of cocktail sauce or lemon rémoulade (or both!). Garnish each with a romaine leaf, a lobster claw, and a lemon wedge.

LOBSTER AVOCADO COCKTAILS

Lobsters are referred to as the "King of Seafood" and are definitely the pride of Atlantic Canada. The meat is delicately textured and succulently flavoured. Here the lobster meat is paired with rich, buttery-smooth avocado.

Serves 4

CLAMS CASINO

Make the best clams casino with this easy recipe. Lots of spicy chorizo sausage, sweet peppers, and tomatoes, plus a topping of Parmesan bread crumbs, give these stuffed clams so much flavour and crunch. They make a fabulous starter for a dinner party. Use littlenecks or cherrystone clams if you can't get your hands on bar clams.

Serves 6

3 large bar clams
1 tbsp (15 mL) unsalted butter
1 small onion, diced
1 clove garlic, minced
2 chorizo sausages, casings removed, crumbled
½ cup (125 mL) diced red and yellow bell peppers
¼ cup (60 mL) white wine
½ cup (125 mL) chopped canned tomatoes
1 tsp (5 mL) chopped thyme
½ cup (125 mL) halved cherry tomatoes
Salt and black pepper
½ cup (125 mL) panko bread crumbs
¼ cup (60 mL) grated Parmesan cheese
1 tbsp (15 mL) chopped parsley
1 tsp (5 mL) chopped chives

Put 2 cups (500 mL) of water in a large pot and salt it. Add the clams, cover the pot, and bring to a boil over high heat. Steam until the clams open, 10 to 15 minutes. Remove the meat from the shells and coarsely chop; set aside the meat and shells.

In a large sauté pan over medium heat, melt the butter. Add the onions and garlic and cook, stirring frequently, until soft. Add the chorizo and peppers and cook, stirring occasionally, until the peppers are soft and the sausage is brown, 3 to 4 minutes. Deglaze with the white wine, then stir in the canned tomatoes, thyme, and clams. Cook until the sauce thickens, about 5 minutes. Remove from heat, stir in the cherry tomatoes, and season with salt and black pepper.

Preheat the broiler. Spread a good layer of coarse salt in a baking sheet to keep the shells level.

Toss together the bread crumbs, Parmesan, parsley, and chives. Spoon the hot clam filling into the reserved shells. Top with the bread crumb mixture to cover the shell. Place the shells on the baking sheet and broil until browned.

For the Tomato Gazpacho

2 lb (1 kg) red beefsteak tomatoes,
    coarsely chopped
2 large yellow bell peppers,
    coarsely chopped
2 English cucumbers, peeled and
    coarsely chopped
1 small red onion, chopped
1 clove garlic, chopped
¾ cup (175 mL) extra-virgin olive oil
¼ cup (60 mL) sherry vinegar
1 tsp (5 mL) hot pepper sauce
Salt and freshly ground black pepper
3 tbsp (50 mL) Herb Pesto (page 253)

For the Devilled Crab Salad

½ lb (250 g) Dungeness crabmeat,
    picked over
½ cup (125 mL) mayonnaise
2 tsp (10 mL) My Old Bay Seasoning
    (page 259)
2 tsp (10 mL) Dijon mustard
2 tbsp (30 mL) finely diced celery
2 tbsp (30 mL) thinly sliced green onion
2 tbsp (30 mL) finely chopped chives
1 cup (250 mL) quartered cherry
    tomatoes
½ cup (125 mL) thinly sliced English
    cucumber
¼ cup (60 mL) finely chopped basil
3 tbsp (50 mL) extra-virgin olive oil
2 tbsp (30 mL) sherry vinegar
Salt and freshly ground black pepper

TOMATO GAZPACHO & CRAB SALAD

Chilled gazpacho is the quintessential summer soup. But the only way this Spanish classic will taste delicious is if you use only the freshest, ripest tomatoes you can find. The spicy crab salad adds a creamy richness to the cool, crisp flavours of the gazpacho.

Serves 6

To make the gazpacho, in a large bowl, stir together the tomatoes, bell peppers, cucumbers, onion, garlic, oil, vinegar, and hot sauce; season with salt and black pepper. Working in batches, purée in a blender until smooth. Transfer to a bowl, cover, and chill for at least 1 hour.

To make the crab salad, in a medium bowl, combine the crabmeat, mayonnaise, my old bay seasoning, mustard, celery, green onions, and chives. Gently mix together until all the ingredients are just combined.

In a small bowl, toss together the cherry tomatoes, cucumber, basil, olive oil, and sherry vinegar. Season well with salt and freshly ground black pepper.

To serve, place a teaspoon of the herb pesto in the bottom of a soup bowl. Spoon the tomato-cucumber salad in the centre of the bowl. Top with the crab salad. Whisk the chilled gazpacho and pour it around the crab salad.

PINK SHRIMP

For my first-ever shrimping adventure, I travelled to postcard-perfect Newport, Oregon, to rediscover the joys of Oregon pink shrimp—those teeny-tiny, butter-sweet, perfectly salty morsels of delight. One great thing I learned is that pink shrimp are sustainably harvested. That's always a requirement for me, as it should be for any fish eater.

I went out to sea with Corey Rock, captain of the *Kylie Lynn*, who took us so far from shore that we had to sleep overnight on his 73-foot beauty of a boat. Even the sleeping quarters were shrimpy. A fisherman's life is not for the faint of heart, quote me on that. In the midst of the considerable chaos, thanks to me, I realized that shrimping is like behind-the-scenes in a restaurant on a Saturday night—it's a slow but steady, relaxed atmosphere that morphs into *here we go*, full steam ahead, all hands on deck for a few hours. On a shrimp boat, you've got to hustle to get those shrimp sorted and on ice fast, because as the deckhands say, "A handful of rotted shrimp don't do us no good."

The two key things to keep in mind when cooking pink shrimp are simplicity and speed. Let the natural flavours shine through. A quickly sautéed pink shrimp is tender and delicious. Use them as a go-to for salads, pastas, and more.

SIZZLING PINK SHRIMP

This quick and easy shrimp dish is loaded with garlic, spiciness, butter, and wine. It's perfect with crusty bread or served over your favourite pasta.

Serves 4 to 6

2 lb (1 kg) pink shrimp, peeled
2 tsp (10 mL) Harissa Paste (page 260)
½ tsp (2 mL) salt
2 tbsp (30 mL) olive oil
3 tbsp (50 mL) unsalted butter

4 cloves garlic, thinly sliced
¼ cup (60 mL) white wine
2 tbsp (30 mL) lemon juice
1 tbsp (15 mL) chopped parsley

In a medium bowl, toss the shrimp with the harissa paste and salt. Set aside.

Heat a large cast-iron skillet over medium-high heat, then add the olive oil. When the oil is hot, add the butter and garlic. Once the butter is nearly melted, add the shrimp and cook, stirring occasionally, until they are cooked through, about 3 minutes.

Add the wine, lemon juice, and parsley, and cook for 30 seconds. Serve immediately with crusty bread.

Here's an idea: Substitute large shrimp, peeled and deveined, for the pink shrimp.

For the Bouillabaisse Relish

2 tbsp (30 mL) extra-virgin olive oil
2 shallots, finely diced
1 clove garlic, grated
¼ cup (60 mL) finely diced carrot
¼ cup (60 mL) finely diced fennel
¼ cup (60 mL) finely diced celery
2 tbsp (30 mL) sherry vinegar
2 tbsp (30 mL) finely chopped basil
Salt and Espelette pepper

For the Shrimp Crostini

1 baguette, cut into slices 1½ inches
   (4 cm) thick
¼ cup (60 mL) olive oil
¼ cup (60 mL) finely chopped parsley
1 clove garlic, minced
Salt and pepper
2 tbsp (30 mL) unsalted butter
2 shallots, finely chopped
1 lb (500 g) pink shrimp, peeled
1 tbsp (15 mL) finely chopped chives
Juice of ½ lemon
Saffron Aïoli (page 251)

PINK SHRIMP CROSTINI

Bouillabaisse is a traditional Provençale fish stew that is flavoured with garlic, herbs, fennel, and saffron. I love these flavours, and for this simple crostini recipe, I have chosen the buttery pink shrimp, which seem to float on top of warm toasted crostini, and let it sail with a bouillabaisse-inspired relish with saffron aïoli.

Serves 4 to 8

To make the relish, heat the olive oil in a small skillet over medium heat. Cook the shallots and garlic, stirring frequently, for 2 minutes. Add the carrot, fennel, and celery and continue to cook for 5 minutes. Remove from heat. Stir in the vinegar and basil. Season with salt and pepper to taste; set aside.

To make the shrimp crostini, preheat your oven to 400°F (200°C). Brush both sides of the baguette slices with some of the olive oil and place on a baking sheet. Bake for 3 minutes, turn over, and bake for a few minutes more, until golden brown. Meanwhile, in a small bowl, combine the remaining olive oil, the parsley, and garlic; season with salt and pepper. Press both sides of the baguette slices into the parsley mixture. Return to the oven and bake for about 2 minutes. Keep warm.

Melt the butter in a large sauté pan over medium-high heat. Add the shallots and cook for 3 minutes or until translucent. Add the shrimp and sauté for 3 minutes or until the shrimp are just cooked. Remove from heat and stir in the chives and lemon juice. Season with salt and pepper.

To serve, place the warm crostini on a platter, then spoon the shrimp on top. Garnish with the bouillabaisse relish and a spoonful of saffron aïoli.

Here's an idea: Large shrimp, diced, would be a perfect substitute for the pink shrimp.

PAN-SEARED SALMON

The simple pleasures of this dish make it one of my favourites: a perfect hollandaise sauce loaded with pink shrimp.

Serves 4

4 skin-on salmon fillets
   (each 6 oz/175 g)
Salt and pepper
2 tbsp (30 mL) olive oil
1 cup (250 mL) warm Hollandaise Sauce
   (page 254)

1 cup (250 mL) pink shrimp,
   cooked and peeled
2 tbsp (30 mL) unsalted butter
1 shallot, finely diced
1 lb (500 g) spinach

Score the salmon skin with a sharp knife. Season the salmon with salt and pepper. Heat the oil in a large, heavy skillet over medium-high heat. Add the salmon, skin side down, and sear until golden brown and crisp, about 4 minutes. Turn fillets over and sear until salmon is just cooked through, about 2 minutes more. Remove salmon from the pan and keep warm.

In a small bowl, combine the hollandaise sauce and pink shrimp. Adjust the seasonings.

In the same skillet, melt the butter over medium-high heat. Add the shallots and cook for about 1 minute. Add the spinach, packing it down. Using a spatula, lift the spinach and turn it over in the pan so that you coat more of it with the buttered shallots. Cover and cook for 1 minute. Uncover and turn the spinach over again. When it is completely wilted, remove from heat. Drain any excess moisture from the pan. Season the spinach with salt and pepper.

Divide the spinach mixture among 4 plates. Place a piece of salmon, skin side up, on top and cover the salmon with a large spoonful of the pink shrimp hollandaise.

CRAB

I have fond memories of eating crab in my youth and in my early years of cooking. The finest crab I have ever tasted was caught in Tofino, B.C. Where food comes from often influences the way it tastes. Flying into Tofino is an overwhelmingly gorgeous experience, with the mountains and ocean all around. And on the ground, the landscape, fishermen, surfers, long-time residents, and new Canadians all come together to make a

unique, beautifully textured city and an ideal place to cook and eat great crab.

Dungeness crab is in season in the Pacific Northwest from mid-November until June. Word on the beach is that what makes Dungeness crabs from Tofino so fantastic is a combination of the strong ocean currents and the clear, clean, cold water. The strong currents make the crabs swim harder, which makes the meat thicker and sweeter than with other kinds of crab, even Dungeness crabs from other places.

CRAB CAKES SALAD

These crab cakes are truly amazing! I must have made them a million times at the Four Seasons Hotel in New York. Plump, sweet crabmeat is the key to making these a hit at any occasion.

Serves 4 to 6

For the Bean, Corn, & Pepper Salad

2 cups (500 mL) green and yellow beans, trimmed
¼ cup (60 mL) olive oil
2 tsp (10 mL) diced shallots
1 clove garlic, minced
1 red chili pepper, seeded and minced
Kernels from 2 ears of corn
1 small red bell pepper, diced
1 yellow bell pepper, diced
Juice of 1 lemon
¼ cup (60 mL) minced chives
Salt and black pepper
2 cups (500 mL) mixed greens, such as celery leaves, arugula, endive, butter lettuce

For the Crab Cakes

¼ cup (60 mL) mayonnaise
3 egg yolks
Juice of 1 lemon
1 tbsp (15 mL) Dijon mustard
1 tsp (5 mL) Worcestershire sauce
1 tsp (5 mL) hot pepper sauce
3 green onions, thinly sliced
2 tbsp (30 mL) finely chopped parsley
2 tbsp (30 mL) finely chopped chives
Salt and pepper
1 lb (500 g) cooked crabmeat, picked over well
⅓ cup (75 mL) panko bread crumbs
2 tbsp (30 mL) olive oil
Lemon Rémoulade (page 252)

To make the salad, cook the beans in a pot of boiling salted water until tender, about 3 minutes. Drain and plunge into a bowl of ice water. Drain again and transfer to a large salad bowl. Meanwhile, in a large sauté pan over medium-high heat, heat the olive oil. Add the shallots, garlic, and chili pepper; cook, stirring, for about 1 minute. Add the corn and red and yellow bell peppers; cook, stirring occasionally, until the corn turns bright yellow. Remove from heat and stir in the lemon juice, chives, and salt and pepper. Add the corn mixture to the beans and toss together well. Set aside.

To make the crab cakes, in a large bowl, whisk together the mayonnaise, egg yolks, lemon juice, mustard, Worcestershire sauce, and hot sauce. Stir in the green onions, parsley, and chives. Season the mixture well with salt and pepper. Fold in the crabmeat until coated thoroughly. Sprinkle the bread crumbs over the mixture and gently mix together. Do not overwork the mixture. Carefully shape into 4 to 6 crab cakes.

Heat the oil in a large nonstick skillet over medium heat. When the oil is hot, add the crab cakes and cook until golden brown on the bottom, 3 to 4 minutes. Carefully flip the crab cakes and cook the other side until golden brown.

Toss the mixed greens with the bean salad and adjust the seasonings. Serve the crab cakes with the salad, and pass the lemon rémoulade separately.

8 oz (250 g) dried Chinese egg noodles
3 tbsp (50 mL) peanut oil
Salt and black pepper
1 tbsp (15 mL) cornstarch
1 tbsp (15 mL) cold water
2 tbsp (30 mL) soy sauce
1 tbsp (15 mL) sugar
1 tbsp (15 mL) sesame oil
2 cloves garlic, minced
2 tbsp (30 mL) grated ginger
1 tsp (5 mL) chili flakes

2 carrots, cut in half lengthwise and then thinly sliced diagonally
1 red bell pepper, cut into thin strips
1 yellow bell pepper, cut into thin strips
1 cup (250 mL) thinly sliced napa cabbage
1 cup (250 mL) snow peas, cut diagonally
2 cups (500 mL) bean sprouts
1 lb (500 g) cooked Dungeness crabmeat, picked over
2 large green onions, thinly sliced

DUNGENESS CRAB STIR-FRY

For crabs, simple is good, but Szechuan is even better. The ginger, the pungent garlic, the fiery peppers, the sweet onions—amazing. I love those flavours any time, but wow, mix them up with some Dungeness crab, and that's a match made in heaven. I came up with the idea for this recipe while sitting on the beach in Tofino with my new surfer friends, eating mouth-watering ginger and green onion crab, cracking open the shells and revealing the juicy meat.

Serves 4

Add noodles to a pot of boiling salted water and cook until just tender but still firm to the bite, about 3 minutes. Drain well and toss with 1 tbsp (15 mL) of the peanut oil. Season with salt and pepper.

Heat a small nonstick pan over medium-high heat. Place a handful of noodles in the pan and flatten with a spatula. Cook for 2 to 3 minutes, until crispy and golden brown on the bottom, then flip and cook until the other side is crispy and golden brown. Drain on paper towels. Repeat with the remaining noodles, making 4 cakes in all.

In a small bowl, stir together the cornstarch and cold water. Stir in the soy sauce, sugar, and sesame oil.

Heat a large sauté pan or wok over high heat. Add 2 tbsp (30 mL) of the peanut oil. Add the garlic, ginger, and chili flakes; sauté for 1 minute. Add the carrots, red and yellow bell peppers, cabbage, snow peas, and bean sprouts. Stir-fry until the carrots are just crisp-tender, about 2 minutes. Add the crabmeat and green onions. Stir the cornstarch mixture and add to the wok. Cook, stirring often, until the sauce thickens, about 2 minutes.

To serve, place a crispy noodle cake on a plate and spoon the crab stir-fry on top.

COOKING LOBSTER

Yes, you can microwave a lobster! In all of my years of cooking, I had never seen this method used until lobster fishermen Frank and Stanton showed me. It was the best lobster I have ever had.

Cooking in the microwave is the fastest way if you are cooking only one lobster. When cooking a lobster in the microwave, you do need to cut off the rubber bands. Put the lobster in a microwave-safe plastic bag and add ¼ cup (60 mL) water, 1 tbsp (15 mL) sea salt, and the juice of half a lemon. Seal the bag. Cook on high heat for 6 minutes per pound (500 g) plus an extra minute for each ¼ lb (125 g). Wait a few minutes until you open the bag—it will be piping hot.

MICROWAVE LOBSTER

1 onion, chopped
1 carrot, quartered
2 stalks celery, quartered
1 lemon, thinly sliced
2 sprigs thyme
8 sprigs parsley

1 bay leaf
1 tsp (5 mL) black peppercorns
Sea salt
2 live lobsters
(each 1¼ to 1½ lb/625 to 750 g)

BOILED LOBSTER

Fill a very large stockpot three-quarters full with cold water. Add the onion, carrot, celery, lemon, thyme, parsley, bay leaf, peppercorns, and a generous amount of sea salt. The water should taste like the ocean. Place over high heat and bring to a rolling boil. Remove the rubber bands from the lobster claws. Plunge the lobsters, one at a time, headfirst into the water. Cook, uncovered, until they turn bright red, about 12 minutes. Use tongs to remove them from the pot and transfer to a bowl of ice water until chilled.

Twist the claws with their knuckles from the body. Separate the knuckles from the claws. Crack the knuckles and claws to open them, and remove the meat; set aside. Grasp the body and tailpiece and twist the tail from the joint where it meets the body. Pull off the tail flippers. Bend the tailpiece back to crack off the end of the shell. Use your fingers to push the tail meat out the flipper end. Remove with a fork and set aside. Discard any remaining lobster.

LOBSTER ROLLS

Lobster rolls are on roadside menus all throughout the Atlantic provinces in the summertime. Lightly buttered toasted rolls are deliciously overstuffed with sweet chunks of lobster tossed with capers and rémoulade sauce. Nothing wrong with that!

Serves 4

4 lobsters, cooked and shelled (page 23), chilled, and cut into bite-size pieces
1 cup (250 mL) mayonnaise
1 tsp (5 mL) lemon juice
1 stalk celery, finely diced
¼ cup (60 mL) chopped celery leaves
2 tbsp (30 mL) chopped dill
1 tbsp (15 mL) capers, chopped
Salt and pepper
4 top-split hot dog rolls
1 tbsp (15 mL) unsalted butter
1 head butter lettuce

In a bowl, combine the lobster meat, mayonnaise, lemon juice, celery, celery leaves, dill, and capers. Fold together gently to mix well. Season with salt and pepper.

Place a large skillet over medium heat. Butter the hot dog rolls and place in the skillet. Toast until golden on each side. Transfer the rolls to a serving plate. Put some lettuce in each roll and divide the lobster mixture among the rolls.

LOBSTER

I travelled to Freeport, Nova Scotia, to eat fresh lobster and to learn how it's fished. I can report back to you that lobster fishing stinks, it's stupid hard, and it's totally worth it. Thankfully, there are lobster fishermen who are tougher than I am, and kind enough to keep us happy with all the lobsters we can eat. I also now believe from my first-hand experience that Bay of Fundy lobsters are among the finest in the world.

Everybody knows that lobster is tasty, but until you have it straight from the sea, you don't really get how crazy great it is. I mean, honestly, think about this: as a chef in New York City, I used to make an omelette with lobster, asparagus, white truffles, and caviar and charge $1000. It was amazing. Yet then I get off a lobster boat in Nova Scotia and there's Stanton Seamore on the dock with just a lobster in a bag of seawater and he pops it in the microwave. It was the best lobster I had ever tasted, as fresh as it gets, simple, and full-on flavour.

FILET MIGNON & LOBSTER MASH

Growing up, I was always in charge of making the mashed potatoes for our family dinners. I guess I must have grown up, because we never had lobster in our mashed potatoes back then! When you want to splurge, try this recipe. My mom says these are the best mashed potatoes she has ever tasted.

Serves 4

For the Lobster Mash

1 lb (500 g) russet potatoes, peeled
    and cut into 2-inch (5 cm) pieces
¾ to 1 cup (175 to 250 mL) whole milk
2 lobsters, cooked and shelled
    (page 23), chilled, and cut into
    bite-size pieces
¼ cup (60 mL) unsalted butter
2 tbsp (30 mL) minced chives
Salt and pepper

For the Filet Mignon

2 tbsp (30 mL) olive oil
4 filets mignons (each 6 oz/175 g)
Salt and pepper
2 thyme sprigs
2 cloves garlic, crushed
3 tbsp (50 mL) unsalted butter
Fleur de sel for finishing

To make the lobster mash, put the potatoes in a large pot of cold salted water and bring to a boil. Cook until the potatoes are tender, about 20 minutes. Meanwhile, bring ½ cup (125 mL) of the milk to a simmer in a medium saucepan. Stir in the lobster meat and set aside. Drain the potatoes, return them to the pot, and mash. Stir in the butter and enough of the remaining milk until the mash is slightly thicker than desired consistency. Add the lobster mixture and chives; combine well. Season with salt and pepper. Set aside and keep warm.

To cook the filets mignons, heat the olive oil in a heavy skillet over high heat. Season the filets with salt and pepper. Sear the filets for 3 to 4 minutes on each side for rare to medium-rare. Add the thyme, garlic, and butter. When the garlicky butter is sizzling, baste the filets, then remove them from the pan. Leave to rest for 1 or 2 minutes before serving.

Divide the lobster mash among 4 plates. Arrange the filets on top of the potatoes. Sprinkle the filets with fleur de sel. Serve with boiled asparagus.

LOBSTER THERMIDOR

Lobster Thermidor is a true classic of French cuisine. It is perceived as an extravagant and indulgent dish that cannot be prepared at home. I disagree and say bring back the classics! I have created an easy version that you will enjoy making and sharing.

Serves 4

2 lobsters (each 1½ lb/750 g), cooked (page 23)
4 tbsp (60 mL) unsalted butter
3 shallots, finely chopped
1 carrot, finely diced
1 stalk celery, finely diced
1 cup (250 mL) button mushrooms, quartered
1 cup (250 mL) dry white wine

1 cup (250 mL) heavy cream
2 tbsp (30 mL) cognac
1 tbsp (15 mL) Dijon mustard
2 tbsp (30 mL) chopped parsley
2 tsp (10 mL) chopped tarragon
½ cup (125 mL) grated Gruyère cheese
Salt and pepper
2 tbsp (30 mL) grated Parmesan cheese

Cut the lobsters in half lengthwise. Remove the meat from the claws and tail. Cut the lobster meat into bite-size pieces. Discard any coral and the meat from the head. Clean out the body shells and set aside.

To prepare the sauce, melt 1 tbsp (15 mL) of the butter in a medium saucepan over medium-low heat. Add the shallots, carrot, and celery and cook until softened, about 2 minutes. Add the mushrooms and continue to cook for 2 to 3 minutes, until the mushrooms are golden. Increase the heat to medium-high. Add the wine and reduce until the liquid has almost evaporated, about 10 minutes.

Add the cream and cook, stirring occasionally, until reduced slightly. Stir in the lobster meat; heat for 2 minutes. Swirl in the remaining butter. Stir in the cognac, mustard, parsley, and tarragon. Remove from heat and stir in half of the Gruyère. Season with salt and pepper.

Preheat the broiler. Divide the lobster sauce between the shells. Sprinkle with the remaining Gruyère and the Parmesan. Broil for 2 to 3 minutes, or until bubbling and golden.

For the Prosciutto Croutons

¼ cup (60 mL) unsalted butter

4 slices prosciutto, diced

2 cups (500 mL) ½-inch (1 cm) cubes
  sourdough bread

1 tsp (5 mL) coarsely cracked
  black pepper

Salt

For the Calamari Salad

2 lb (1 kg) small squid

3 cups (750 mL) vegetable oil

½ cup (125 mL) all-purpose flour

2 tsp (10 mL) salt

½ tsp (2 mL) baking soda

1 tsp (5 mL) chili flakes

1 tbsp (15 mL) freshly cracked black
  pepper

1 cup (250 mL) milk

2 heads frisée, trimmed

2 heads radicchio, cut into strips

½ cup (125 mL) peeled English cucumber
  cut into thin half-moons

1 cup (250 mL) cherry tomatoes,
  cut in half

¼ cup (60 mL) thinly sliced radishes

¼ cup (60 mL) Basil Sun-Dried Tomato
  Vinaigrette (page 257)

CRISPY CALAMARI SALAD

The crispy fried calamari and the prosciutto croutons are the stars of this salad. They add an amazing salty-peppery crunch to this fresh Californian-inspired salad tossed with lots of basil sun-dried tomato vinaigrette.

Serves 4 to 6

To make the prosciutto croutons, preheat your oven to 350°F (180°C). In a large, heavy skillet over medium heat, melt the butter. Stir in the prosciutto and cook for 3 minutes. Add the bread and pepper and stir to coat. Spread out the bread cubes on a baking sheet. Sprinkle with salt. Bake until the croutons are golden, stirring occasionally, about 5 minutes. (The croutons can be made ahead of time and set aside.)

To clean the squid, grip the head in one hand and the body in the other. Gently pull the head away from the body. The cuttlebone and innards should come right along with the head; discard these. The tentacles are perfectly edible. Sever them from the head just below the eyes. Remove and discard the beak from the centre of the tentacles. The outer coloured skin can be scraped or rubbed from the body tube under running water, leaving the white meat. Rinse meat and tentacles inside and out under cold running water. Cut the bodies into ¼-inch (5 mm) rings.

In a deep, heavy sauté pan or pot, heat the oil to 375°F (190°C). Sift the flour, salt, and baking soda into a medium bowl. Stir in the chili flakes and black pepper. Place the milk in a shallow bowl. Dip the prepared calamari into the milk, then into the flour mixture, turning to coat. Shake off excess flour. Fry in batches until golden brown and crispy, 2 to 3 minutes. Drain on paper towels. Season with salt and pepper.

In a large salad bowl, combine the frisée, radicchio, cucumber, tomatoes, and radishes. Toss with the vinaigrette. Top the salad with the prosciutto croutons and calamari.

SQUID

I've known the bright lights of the Big Apple and the glitter of Tinseltown, but I've never experienced anything quite like the otherworldly glow of the lights off a squid boat deep out in the Pacific Ocean at night.

Squid fishing is a unique process. Miles of nets gather up tons of squid as they rise to the surface to see the light that comes from huge, stadium-style lights rigged onto these boats. You know that feeling when in real life you all of a sudden feel like you're on a movie set because everything looks big and surreal and full of special effects? Being out on the ocean in the black of night catching squid is like that—it looks like something out of a sci-fi movie.

But squid is an amazing food. It's incredibly versatile—you can fry it, steam it, sauté it, stuff it, and roast it, and it's always going to come out beautiful. Just don't overcook it (I think I'm developing a running theme here—basically, don't overcook anything). The other great thing about squid is how sustainable it is. It's not always easy to be sure you're eating seafood responsibly in today's market, but with California market squid and Atlantic longfin squid, you're on safe ground. So, enjoy, savour, and get cooking, worry-free.

STUFFED CALAMARI WITH RISOTTO

Squid seems to have been created for stuffing. Calamari stuffed with pancetta and veal is moist and delicious and so easy to make. The gorgeously dark and deliciously comforting risotto is a traditional Venetian version that has always been a favourite of mine. More importantly, this is the kind of dish that you can make over and over again, for yourself or for friends, without ever tiring of it.

Serves 4

For the Stuffed Calamari
2 tbsp (30 mL) olive oil
½ onion, finely chopped
¼ cup (60 mL) finely diced pancetta
1 tbsp (15 mL) roughly chopped thyme
1 large egg
1 lb (500 g) ground veal
½ cup (125 mL) panko bread crumbs
¼ cup (60 mL) whole milk
Salt and pepper
4 medium squid, cleaned (see page 31)
½ cup (125 mL) fish stock (page 247)

For the Squid Ink Risotto
4 to 5 cups (1 to 1.25 L) fish stock
½ cup (125 mL) unsalted butter
½ cup (125 mL) olive oil
3 shallots, finely chopped
1½ cups (375 mL) arborio rice
1 cup (250 mL) dry white wine
2 tsp (10 mL) squid ink paste
Salt and pepper
2 tbsp (30 mL) grated Parmesan cheese for garnish

For the Creamy Leek Sauce
2 tbsp (30 mL) unsalted butter
2 large leeks (white part only), diced
1 cup (250 mL) heavy cream
Salt and pepper

To make the stuffed calamari, in a large skillet over medium heat, heat 1 tbsp (15 mL) of the olive oil. Add the onion, pancetta, and thyme; cook, stirring frequently, until the onions are caramelized, 8 to 10 minutes. Set aside. In a large bowl, beat the egg. Add the ground veal, bread crumbs, milk, onion mixture, and salt and pepper to taste. Mix together well. Carefully stuff each squid body with the veal mixture; pat squid to distribute the filling evenly. Weave a wooden pick horizontally across the wide opening of each squid to seal. Set aside.

To make the squid ink risotto, in a large saucepan bring the fish stock to a gentle simmer. In another large saucepan over medium-low heat, melt the butter with the olive oil. Add the shallots and cook for a few minutes until softened but not coloured. Add the rice and stir with a wooden spoon until the rice is translucent and coated with the oil. Add the wine and cook until the liquid has reduced by half. Add the squid ink and stir thoroughly with a wooden spoon to disperse the ink throughout the rice. Add the stock, a ladleful at a time, stirring until each addition is absorbed before adding more. This should take about 20 minutes. Season to your taste with salt and pepper.

Meanwhile, make the leek sauce. Melt the butter in a large, heavy skillet over medium-low heat. Add the leeks and cook until tender, about 8 minutes. Add the cream and simmer until slightly thickened, about 3 minutes. Season to taste with salt and pepper. Remove from heat and keep warm.

About halfway through cooking the risotto, finish the squid. In a large, heavy skillet over medium-high heat, heat the remaining 1 tbsp (15 mL) of olive oil. Sauté the squid, turning once, until browned. Reduce heat to medium-low. Add the fish stock, cover, and simmer until the squid is tender and cooked all the way through, about 8 minutes. Remove from stock, remove the wooden picks, and thickly slice the squid.

To serve, divide the squid ink risotto among 4 large pasta bowls. Ladle a good spoonful of creamy leeks on top of the risotto and top with sliced stuffed calamari. Sprinkle with Parmesan.

MUSSELS WITH THAI CURRY

This fragrant Thai dish with lemongrass-scented mussels in a coconut-laced red curry sauce is sure to get your taste buds into action. Years ago, Chef Ian Chalermkittichai taught me how to make this incredible seasoning salt using jasmine rice, ginger, and peppercorns and it brings amazing flavour to the mussels. I use this seasoning trick on everything. Try it on grilled steaks, chicken, and fish.

Serves 6

For the Lemongrass-Skewered Mussels

¼ cup (60 mL) jasmine rice
1 tbsp (15 mL) pink peppercorns
1 tsp (5 mL) finely grated ginger
1 tsp (5 mL) grated orange zest
1 tsp (5 mL) kosher salt
3 stalks lemongrass, cut in half lengthwise and trimmed to 6 inches (15 cm) long
2 tbsp (30 mL) unsalted butter
Salt and pepper

For the Thai Vegetable Curry

3 tbsp (50 mL) vegetable oil
2 cups (500 mL) peeled sweet potato cut into 1-inch (2.5 cm) cubes
1 red onion, diced
2 stalks celery, thinly sliced diagonally
1 leek (white and pale green parts only), diced
1 red bell pepper, diced
1 tbsp (15 mL) minced garlic
¼ cup (60 mL) Thai red curry paste
6 kaffir lime leaves
¼ cup (60 mL) fish sauce
2 cans (each 14 oz/398 mL) unsweetened coconut milk
2 lb (1 kg) mussels, scrubbed and debearded
½ cup (125 mL) chopped cilantro
3 cups (750 mL) cooked jasmine rice
Salt and pepper

To make the jasmine and pink peppercorn crust for the skewered mussels, preheat your oven to 325°F (160°C). Toss together the jasmine rice, pink peppercorns, ginger, orange zest, and salt. Spread on a baking sheet. Bake, stirring occasionally, for 20 minutes or until the rice is toasted and fragrant. Grind in a spice grinder. Set aside.

To make the vegetable curry, in a large stockpot, heat the oil over medium heat. Add the sweet potato, onions, celery, leeks, and bell peppers; cook, stirring, until the onions and celery are softened, about 5 minutes. Stir in the garlic and cook until fragrant. Stir in the curry paste and lime leaves and cook for 1 minute. Stir in the fish sauce and coconut milk; bring to a boil. Lower the heat and simmer for 5 minutes. Add the mussels, cover, and cook until the mussels open, about 5 minutes. Stir in the cilantro, cover, and remove from heat. Let the curry sit for 1 minute. Remove the mussels from their shells and set aside. Discard any mussels that didn't open.

Skewer 4 to 6 mussels onto each lemongrass stalk. Return any remaining mussels to the curry. Dust the skewered mussels generously with the jasmine and pink peppercorn dust. In a large skillet over medium-high heat, melt the butter. Add the skewers and cook for about 1 minute on each side.

Divide the cooked rice among serving bowls. Spoon the vegetable curry over the rice. Top each serving with the skewered mussels.

IN THE POND

CRAWFISH

Crawfish, crayfish, mudbugs, crawdaddies, yabbies—it doesn't matter what you call them, these little crustaceans are the heart and soul of Louisiana bayou cooking. When I was in Rayne, Louisiana, trying my hand at crawfish farming was one of the most challenging adventures I've ever had. Everything bites—the crawfish, the crabs, the bees, the bugs, and even that steamy, sweltering southern heat.

Get through it all, though, and something tasty is waiting for you on the other side. Louisiana bayou cooking is famous for dishes like buttery-rich étouffée, spicy boiled crawfish, crispy fried catfish, and except for the holy trinity (that's bell peppers, onions, and celery for you non-Cajuns) and some okra, not a vegetable to be seen.

I have to admit I was a little daunted by the prospect of cooking fresh, bright food for these deep-fried southern guys, but in the end I rose to the challenge. I didn't really have a choice! Down-home, simple food is forever king in Rayne, but I think I showed everyone that broadening their food experience can only be a good thing. I even got the young one, Mills (who recalled the last vegetable he could remember eating was a *grape* …), to eat a vegetable! He didn't like it, but he ate it. And you know, that's something.

CATFISH & SLAW

Most people think of catfish either fried or baked, so I wanted to create a dish that would change people's minds about how they prepare this stereotyped fish. Catfish is mild in flavour and texture, perfect for marinating and served as ceviche. The fresh lemon juice and pickled jalapeños work perfectly with its subtle, sweet flavour. This is fantastic with the deep-fried pickles pictured here (see page 44 for the recipe).

Serves 4

For the Catfish
12 oz (375 g) fresh catfish fillets, skinned, thinly sliced, and well chilled
1 or 2 pickled jalapeño peppers, thinly sliced
2 tbsp (30 mL) pickled jalapeño juice
Juice of 1 lemon
2 tbsp (30 mL) extra-virgin olive oil
1 bunch chives, finely chopped
Sea salt and freshly ground black pepper

For the Slaw
½ cabbage, finely shredded
1 small bunch radishes, julienned
2 green onions, thinly sliced
1 small bunch dill, roughly chopped
2 tbsp (30 mL) chopped parsley
Juice of 2 lemons
¼ cup (60 mL) olive oil
Salt and pepper

Arrange the catfish slices on 4 chilled salad plates. In a bowl, stir together the jalapeños, pickled jalapeño juice, lemon juice, olive oil, and chives. Season with salt and pepper. Spoon the dressing over the catfish. Marinate, refrigerated, for 10 minutes before serving.

Meanwhile, make the slaw. In a large bowl, toss together the cabbage, radishes, green onions, dill, and parsley. Pour the lemon juice and oil over the salad, season with salt and pepper, and toss well.

To serve, top the catfish with the slaw.

Here's an idea: You can substitute any firm salmon or scallops for the catfish.

DEEP-FRIED PICKLES

These deep-fried pickles are a surefire hit when served with Catfish & Slaw (see page 42 for the recipe). They're also great with burgers and grilled cheese sandwiches.

Serves 6

1½ cups (375 mL) all-purpose flour
1 tsp (5 mL) salt
½ tsp (2 mL) black pepper
2 eggs
1 cup (250 mL) milk
1 tbsp (15 mL) Worcestershire sauce
1 tsp (5 mL) hot pepper sauce

1½ cups (375 mL) cornmeal
6 large dill pickles, sliced into ¼-inch
    (5 mm) coins
Vegetable oil for frying
    (about 4 cups/1 L)
Lemon Rémoulade (page 252)

Set 3 shallow bowls next to one another. In the first one, combine the flour, salt, and pepper. In the second, whisk together the eggs, milk, Worcestershire sauce, and hot sauce. Put the cornmeal in the last bowl.

Working with a few slices at a time, toss the pickle slices in the flour, then transfer them to a sieve and shake off the excess flour. Coat the pickles in the egg mixture. Remove them using a slotted spoon and put them in the cornmeal; toss well. Arrange the breaded pickles on a baking sheet lined with waxed paper. Chill for at least 30 minutes.

Heat the oil in a large, heavy pot over high heat until it reaches 350°F (180°C). Working in batches so you don't crowd the pot, carefully add the breaded pickles to the hot oil. Fry for 3 to 4 minutes or until golden brown. Use a slotted spoon to transfer them to paper towels to drain. Sprinkle with salt. Serve with lemon rémoulade.

¼ lb (125 g) bacon, cut into ½-inch (1 cm) pieces
2 tbsp (30 mL) unsalted butter
1 large white onion, finely chopped
2 cloves garlic, roughly chopped
2 stalks celery, finely chopped
2 carrots, diced
1 tsp (5 mL) chili flakes
2 tbsp (30 mL) all-purpose flour

1 red bell pepper, diced
1 yellow bell pepper, diced
1 can (28 oz/796 mL) diced tomatoes
4 cups (1 L) fish stock or vegetable stock (page 247)
1 lb (500 g) crawfish tail meat
Salt and black pepper
1 tbsp (15 mL) chopped parsley
2 green onions, thinly sliced

SPICY CRAWFISH TOMATO CHOWDER

Chowder recipes date back to the sixteenth century. By now, you can only imagine how many different recipes are out there. Originally, chowders were cooked in large pots and meant to feed lots of people whenever they were hungry. So today, take one of the most popular versions, the "Manhattan style" chowder that uses a rich tomato broth, add crawfish and bacon, and invite friends over for dinner.

Serves 4 to 6

In a heavy pot over medium-high heat, cook the bacon until the fat is rendered. Add the butter, onions, garlic, celery, carrots, and chili flakes. Cook, stirring occasionally, until the vegetables are softened, about 5 minutes. Sprinkle the flour over the mixture and stir together well. Cook, stirring, for 3 minutes. Add the bell peppers, tomatoes, and stock. Bring to a boil, then reduce heat and simmer, stirring frequently, until the chowder thickens slightly. Stir in the crawfish. Taste and adjust seasoning.

To serve, ladle chowder into bowls and sprinkle with parsley and green onions. Serve with crawfish beignets on the side.

Here's an idea: Shrimp or lobster may be substituted for the crawfish. Use large peeled and deveined shrimp, chopped into roughly ½-inch (1 cm) pieces, or similarly-sized pieces of lobster.

4 cups (1 L) vegetable oil for deep-frying
2 eggs
1 cup (250 mL) peeled crawfish tails,
      or peeled and deveined shrimp,
      chopped
1 tbsp (15 mL) My Old Bay Seasoning
      (page 259)
1 bunch green onions, thinly sliced

1 clove garlic, minced
1½ cups (375 mL) sifted all-purpose flour
1 tsp (5 mL) baking powder
Salt
½ cup (125 mL) milk
Sea salt and pepper
Cajun Mayonnaise (page 250)

CRAWFISH BEIGNETS

These little crawfish fritters are also a great starter. The tender, succulent crawfish is spiced up and folded into a light batter, then fried until golden brown and crispy on the outside, warm and tender on the inside. The Cajun Mayo is slightly spicy and a perfect accompaniment. You won't be able to eat just eat one—they are addictive.

Makes 16 to 20 beignets

In a large, heavy saucepan, heat the oil over medium-high heat to 350°F (180°C). In a large bowl, whisk the eggs until frothy. Sprinkle the crawfish tails with my old bay seasoning and add to the eggs. Stir in the green onions, garlic, flour, baking powder, salt to taste, and milk. The mixture should be like a thick pancake batter.

Working in batches, use a large tablespoon to carefully drop the beignet mixture into the hot oil. Fry until crispy and golden brown, about 3 minutes. Using a slotted spoon, remove the beignets and drain on paper towels. Sprinkle with sea salt and serve with the mayonnaise.

Here's an idea: You can use large shrimp, peeled and deveined, in place of crawfish.

OYSTERS

To me, oysters always have the feel of a treat about them—something special. Raised in clean, clear water, oysters are an amazing food. I have a long list of favourite varieties—the Blue Points, Malpeques, Cotuits, Wellfleets, tiny Kumamotos, and one of my newfound favourites, Choptank Sweets. It doesn't get any easier than eating them on the half shell plain and simple, with a dash of Tabasco or with some fresh horseradish or with a squeeze of lemon.

The Chesapeake Bay is one of the world's great seafood waters, and oysters and crabs are its signature. Today, most of the oysters in the market from the Chesapeake are farmed. And that's a job and a half, I can tell you first-hand! Huge, and I mean *huge*, rafts of oysters float in the shallow waters before being dragged to shore, where they're cleaned off and the oysters are sorted by hand and packed up for shipping. What makes the process so trying, to put it mildly, is that an oyster float is teeming with gross, wiggly, crawly sea life of all kinds. But the oysters are worth it.

Fresh or roasted, in soup or in stuffing, fried in a sandwich or smoked on steaks, they can hold their own. Thumbs up from me!

OYSTERS FOUR WAYS

Whenever I am travelling on the coastlines, I order oysters. Raw oysters are regarded like wines, as they have complex flavours that vary greatly among varieties and regions. Oysters are amazing, any way you serve them. Here are four recipes I make using Choptank Sweets from the Chesapeake Bay located on Maryland's shore. These oysters are fantastic, robust, and meaty with a clean, crisp finish.

OYSTER CAESAR SHOOTERS

Serves 6

1 cup (250 mL) ice cubes
1 cup (250 mL) Clamato juice
1 tsp (5 mL) lemon juice
1 tsp (5 mL) grated fresh horseradish
3 dashes Worcestershire sauce
2 dashes hot pepper sauce
½ tsp (2 mL) celery salt
Freshly ground black pepper
6 oysters, shucked
3 small celery hearts with leaves,
    cut in half lengthwise
6 lemon wedges

Rim 6 shooter glasses with celery salt. In a bar shaker, combine the ice cubes, Clamato juice, lemon juice, horseradish, Worcestershire sauce, hot sauce, celery salt, and pepper; stir well. Place 1 shucked oyster in each shot glass. Divide the Caesar mixture among the glasses. Garnish each glass with a celery heart and a lemon wedge.

OYSTERS FEAST

Makes 6 oysters

1 seedless orange
1 tbsp (15 mL) rice wine vinegar
1 tsp (5 mL) finely chopped cilantro
1 green onion, thinly sliced

¼ tsp (1 mL) grated ginger
Salt and freshly ground black pepper
6 oysters, shucked and on the half shell

Using a knife, cut the skin and pith away from the orange. Working over a bowl to catch the juices, cut the orange segments from between their membranes. Set aside the segments. Squeeze the membranes to extract any juice. Cut the orange segments into ¼-inch (5 mm) pieces.

To the orange juice, add the rice wine vinegar, cilantro, green onion, and ginger. Whisk to combine. Stir in the orange pieces and season with salt and pepper. Spoon the mixture over each of the shucked oysters.

2 slices bacon, cut into lardons
1 small leek (white part only), finely diced
1 cup (250 mL) spinach
½ cup (125 mL) heavy cream
Salt and pepper
6 oysters, shucked and on the half shell
¼ cup (60 mL) grated Parmesan cheese

BAKED OYSTERS LYNNA-FELLER

Makes 6 oysters

Preheat your oven to 375°F (190°C). Spread a good layer of rock salt in a baking sheet so the oysters will sit securely in the pan.

In a sauté pan over medium-high heat, fry the bacon until golden brown. Add the leeks and cook, stirring often, until softened, about 5 minutes. Stir in the spinach and cream; cook until the cream thickens. Remove from heat and season with salt and pepper.

Place a spoonful of the mixture on top of each oyster. Place the oysters on the baking sheet and sprinkle with the Parmesan. Bake for 5 minutes or until bubbling and cheese is golden brown.

CRISPY FRIED OYSTERS WITH SALSA

Makes 6 oysters

For the Corn Cilantro Salsa
½ cup (125 mL) corn kernels, cooked
¼ red bell pepper, finely chopped
1 green onion, thinly sliced
1 tbsp (15 mL) finely chopped cilantro
1 tsp (5 mL) lime juice
1 tsp (5 mL) white wine vinegar
Salt and freshly ground black pepper
    to taste

For the Corn Purée
1 tbsp (15 mL) unsalted butter
1 shallot, finely chopped
½ cup (125 mL) corn kernels
¼ cup (60 mL) chicken stock (page 245)
Salt and pepper

For the Crispy Fried Oysters
¼ cup (60 mL) all-purpose flour
¼ cup (60 mL) buttermilk
1 large egg
¼ cup (60 mL) cornmeal
6 oysters, shucked
½ cup (125 mL) vegetable oil
6 oyster half shells, cleaned

To make the corn salsa, in a small bowl, combine all the salsa ingredients. Set aside.

To make the corn purée, in a medium saucepan over medium heat, melt the butter. Add the shallots and cook, stirring frequently, until softened. Add the corn and chicken stock. Cook for 8 to 10 minutes, until most of the liquid has evaporated. Transfer the corn to a blender and blend until smooth. Season with salt and pepper. Set aside and keep warm.

To make the crispy fried oysters, set 3 shallow bowls next to one another. Put the flour in the first one. In the second, use a fork to whisk the egg into the buttermilk. Put the cornmeal in the last bowl. Working with 1 oyster at a time, dredge the oysters in the flour, shaking to remove excess flour. Dip the oyster into the egg mixture, then roll in the cornmeal. Set a large sauté pan over medium heat and add the oil. Heat the oil to 375°F (190°C). Add the oysters and fry, turning once, until golden brown, about 1 minute on each side. Remove the oysters with a slotted spoon and drain on paper towels.

To serve, place 1 tsp (5 mL) of corn purée in each oyster shell. Top with 1 tsp (5 mL) of the corn salsa. Place a fried oyster on top of the salsa.

CATFISH

Some fish are just made to be farmed, and catfish is the king of them all. With their big whiskers and serpent-like appearance, catfish are by no means a pretty species. On top of that, they've got a bad reputation for having an unappetizing muddy or musty taste. But when you get a really good, well-raised, farmed catfish, then clean, clean, clean, and delicious is what you're going to taste.

And that mild, sweet taste is worth it. With fresh, farm-raised catfish, you can't beat southern-fried as a cooking method. The batter is crisp; the fish is flaky and moist. Simple is best in this case.

I went to the northwest Florida Panhandle, to a place called Walnut Creek, to see how catfish were raised and to do a little hands-on farming. Picture this, if you will: I'm dressed in neoprene hip waders, stuck inside a small netted "sock" that's filled with thousands of catfish. I won't deny they are some creepy, slimy, out-and-out scary-bad, otherworldly-looking fish. But hey, I try not to judge a book by its cover, and we made memories.

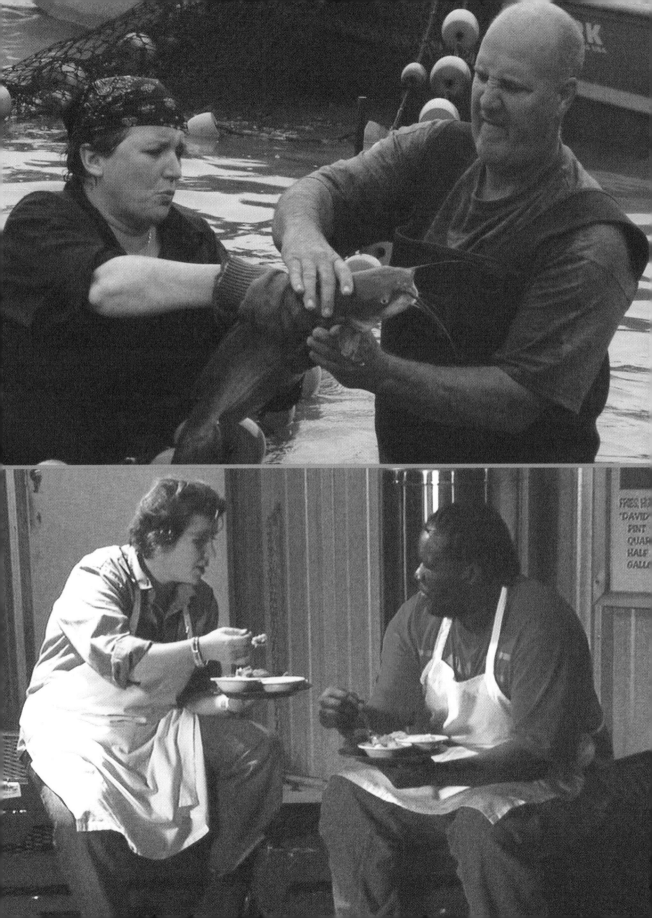

CATFISH IN PARCH-MENT

When I first starting cooking, I was absolutely amazed by the simplicity of this classic French technique: fish with vegetables and aromatic flavours steamed in a parchment envelope, called a papillote. Everything cooks beautifully together in their own juices, giving the fish such wonderful flavour. This is such an easy way to prepare any fish, and once you try it you may never go back to using a pan.

Serves 4

½ cup (125 mL) thinly sliced button
   mushrooms
1 zucchini, julienned
1 small fennel bulb, finely julienned
1 red bell pepper, julienned
1 yellow bell pepper, julienned
½ red onion, thinly sliced lengthwise
1 tbsp (15 mL) olive oil
Salt and black pepper
4 skinless catfish fillets
   (each 6 oz/175 g)

4 tbsp (60 mL) unsalted butter,
   cut into 4 pieces
1 small bunch dill, chopped
¼ cup (60 mL) dry white wine
Juice of 1 lemon
2 tbsp (30 mL) unsalted butter, melted,
   to seal parchment paper
Mousseline Sauce (page 254)

Preheat your oven to 425°F (220°C). In a bowl, combine the mushrooms, zucchini, fennel, red and yellow bell peppers, and onion. Add the oil, season with salt and pepper to taste, and toss.

Cut 4 (12- × 15-inch/30 × 38 cm) sheets of parchment paper. Fold each sheet crosswise in half to make a crease, then unfold. Season the fish with salt and pepper; put 1 fillet to the right of the crease on each parchment sheet. Top each fillet with a quarter of the vegetables, 1 tbsp (15 mL) of the butter, a quarter of the dill, 1 tbsp (15 mL) of the wine, and some lemon juice. Working with 1 package at a time, brush the edges of the parchment with melted butter, then fold the left half of the parchment over the fish. Starting at one corner of the crease, crimp the edges by folding the edge of the parchment over in small triangles (each should overlap the previous one), following a semicircular path around the fillet. Smooth out the folds as you go and tuck the last fold under to seal the papillote completely.

Put papillotes on a baking sheet and bake until they puff up, 10 to 12 minutes. To serve, transfer the packets to 4 plates. With a knife, slit the top of each packet and tear it to expose the fish. Serve with mousseline sauce.

Here's an idea: You can substitute white flaky fish such as halibut, cod, pickerel or snapper for the catfish.

PASTA JAMBALAYA

I've always loved jambalaya for its deep, smoky, spicy deliciousness. This recipe is a twist on an old southern classic: Creole cooking and crayfish meet Italian angel hair pasta.

Serves 4

2 tbsp (30 mL) olive oil
½ lb (250 g) andouille sausage, diced
¼ cup (60 mL) finely chopped yellow onion
1 tbsp (15 mL) minced garlic
1 zucchini, diced
1 red bell pepper, diced
1 can (28 oz/796 mL) diced tomatoes
1 tbsp (15 mL) thyme leaves

½ cup (125 mL) heavy cream
1 lb (500 g) cooked crawfish tails
4 tbsp (60 mL) chopped basil
1 lb (500 g) angel hair pasta
1 tsp (5 mL) My Old Bay Seasoning (page 259)
½ cup (125 mL) grated Parmesan cheese
Salt and pepper

Heat the oil in a large sauté pan over medium-high heat. Add the sausage and onions; cook, stirring occasionally, until the sausage is lightly caramelized and the onions are translucent. Stir in the garlic, then add the zucchini, bell peppers, tomatoes, and thyme. Cook for 5 minutes or until the zucchini and peppers are tender. Stir in the cream and cook an additional 5 minutes. Stir in the crawfish and 2 tbsp (30 mL) of the basil. Keep warm while the pasta cooks.

Add the pasta to a large pot of boiling salted water. Cook until nearly al dente, about 8 minutes. Drain, then immediately toss the pasta with the sauce. Season with my old bay seasoning and mix together well. Season with salt and pepper to taste. Divide among 4 serving bowls, and garnish with the remaining basil and the Parmesan.

Here's an idea: Shrimp can be used instead of crawfish and it's just as good.

CRAWFISH ÉTOUFFÉE

Étouffée is a Cajun one-pot dish most popular in New Orleans and the bayou country of Louisiana. The base of a good étouffée is a dark roux and the "holy trinity," onions, green peppers, and celery. It only gets better when you add the crawfish!

Serves 4

¼ cup (60 mL) unsalted butter
½ cup (125 mL) all-purpose flour
1 cup (250 mL) finely chopped onion
1 cup (250 mL) finely diced celery
½ cup (125 mL) diced green bell pepper
½ cup (125 mL) diced red bell pepper
2 cloves garlic, minced
1 tbsp (15 mL) Cajun Seasoning (page 259)
½ tsp (2 mL) chili flakes
1 bottle (12 oz/341 mL) dark beer
3 cups (750 mL) chicken broth
1 lb (500 g) crawfish, peeled and deveined
¼ cup (60 mL) chopped parsley
4 green onions, finely chopped
Salt and pepper

Melt the butter in a large cast-iron skillet over medium-low heat. Stir in the flour and cook, stirring, until the roux is light brown and has the consistency of peanut butter. Be patient—this will take at least 20 minutes.

Add the onions, celery, green and red bell peppers, and garlic; cook, stirring occasionally, until just tender, 2 to 3 minutes. Stir in the Cajun seasoning and chili flakes; cook for 1 minute. Stir in the beer and broth; simmer for 10 minutes. Add the crawfish tails and parsley. Cover the pot and simmer for 5 minutes. Season to taste with salt and pepper.

Serve over white rice with an icy-cold beer.

1 tbsp (15 mL) unsalted butter
3 tbsp (50 mL) olive oil
1 small onion, finely chopped
2 cloves garlic, finely chopped
3 stalks celery, diced
½ cup (125 mL) diced potatoes
½ cup (125 mL) quartered button
    mushrooms
¼ cup (60 mL) diced leeks
    (white part only)
¼ cup (60 mL) diced carrots
¼ cup (60 mL) all-purpose flour
1 cup (250 mL) white wine
3 cups (750 mL) fish stock (page 247)

1 cup (250 mL) heavy cream
1 lb (500 g) rockfish or similar white fish,
    skinned and cut into 1-inch
    (2.5 cm) cubes
2 dozen oysters, shucked
1 tbsp (15 mL) chopped parsley
1 tbsp (15 mL) chopped thyme
1 tbsp (15 mL) chopped chives
Juice of 1 lemon
Salt and pepper
1 pkg (411 g) frozen puff pastry dough,
    thawed
1 egg, beaten

OYSTER & ROCKFISH POT PIE

This New England–inspired pot pie, loaded with flaky rockfish and plump oysters swimming in a creamy velouté topped with a deep golden puff pastry crust, is a dream come true. Turn the page and see what I mean!

Serves 6

Preheat your oven to 400°F (200°C). In a large saucepan over medium-high heat, melt the butter with the oil. Sauté the onions, garlic, celery, potatoes, mushrooms, leeks, and carrots for 8 minutes. Add the flour to the vegetables and stir to coat well, then add the wine. Reduce heat to medium and cook, stirring, for 3 minutes. Add the stock and cream; stir until smooth. Reduce heat to low and simmer for 15 minutes or until the vegetables are tender. Add the fish and simmer for 5 minutes. Remove from heat. Stir in the oysters, parsley, thyme, chives, lemon juice, and salt and pepper to taste.

Divide the mixture among 6 large ovenproof ramekins. Roll out puff pastry and cut into 6 rounds, making sure they are about ¾ inch (2 cm) larger in diameter than a ramekin. Lay the puff pastry rounds over the ramekins and press against the sides to seal. Brush the tops with the beaten egg. Bake for 15 minutes or until golden brown.

Here's an idea: You can substitute snapper or any flaky fish for rockfish.

LOUISIANA CRAWFISH BOIL

In Louisiana, when it's time to party with lots of friends and family, it's time to start the boil. Leave your conventional rules of dining etiquette in the cutlery drawer. Instead, grab an ice-cold beer, pull up to the picnic table lined with newspaper, and patiently wait for the main attraction—steaming-hot and spicy crawfish. A Cajun tradition!

Serves 8

2 lemons, cut in half
2 bottles (each 12 oz/341 mL) beer
4 sprigs thyme
3 bay leaves
½ tsp (2 mL) cayenne pepper
1 tbsp (15 mL) salt
½ cup (125 mL) My Old Bay Seasoning (page 259)
2 lb (1 kg) red new potatoes, cut in half
3 onions, quartered
4 ears of corn, cut in half crosswise
4 andouille sausages, cut into 2-inch (5 cm) pieces
4 lb (2 kg) fresh crawfish or jumbo shrimp, in shells
Lemon wedges, Cocktail Sauce (page 255), mayonnaise (page 250), and French bread, for serving

Fit a large stockpot with a basket insert and add 4 quarts (4 L) water. Do not fill the pot more than halfway. Squeeze the lemons and add the juice and the squeezed halves to the water. Add the beer, thyme, bay leaves, cayenne pepper, salt, and my old bay seasoning. Cover and bring to a boil, then reduce heat and simmer for 10 minutes to get all the flavours into the boil.

Increase the heat to high and add the potatoes and onions; cook, uncovered, for 15 minutes. Add the corn and sausage; cook for 5 minutes. Add the crawfish, turn off the heat, cover the pot, and let the crawfish steep for 15 minutes. Drain.

To serve, spread the crawfish, sausage, corn, potatoes, and onions out on a newspaper-covered table. Serve with lemon wedges, cocktail sauce, mayonnaise, French bread, and plenty of napkins.

3 tbsp (50 mL) Cajun Seasoning
(page 259)
4 skinless catfish fillets
(each 5 oz/150 g)
2 tbsp (30 mL) canola oil
1 tbsp (15 mL) unsalted butter
1 baguette, cut into 4 and cut in half
lengthwise

¼ cup (60 mL) Lemon Mustard
Rémoulade (page 252)
1 small head iceberg lettuce, finely
shredded
1 beefsteak tomato, sliced
2 dill pickles, thinly sliced

BLACKENED CATFISH PO' BOY

This traditional sandwich from Louisiana is one of my favourites. There are so many versions of the po' boy, which is French bread stuffed with fried shrimp, oysters, soft-shell crabs, or crawfish. My version is all about hot, flaky catfish fillets that are spiced up with a homemade Cajun rub. The best way to eat a po' boy is "all dressed" with lots of rémoulade sauce.

Serves 4

Sprinkle the Cajun seasoning over both sides of the catfish, coating them well. Heat the oil and butter in a large skillet over medium-high heat. Sauté the catfish until just cooked through, about 4 minutes on each side. Transfer to a plate.

Spread both halves of the baguette with lots of rémoulade sauce. Layer with lettuce, tomato, pickles, and the catfish on top.

Here's an idea: Oysters or shrimp can be substituted for the catfish.

IN THE FIELD

FOREST, & BOG

MUSHROOMS

The Oregon coast is incredibly beautiful and, at the same time, incredibly wet. My adventure to the West Coast started with a mushroom forager named Lee Gray, who likes to call himself the Godfarmer, as in God plants it, he harvests it. Lee took me through the woods along the most frightening, nerve-rattling, life-endangering precipice I have ever seen to a remote spot where we foraged for mushrooms. We scoured the forest and found lobster, oyster, matsutake, and chanterelle mushrooms. The good thing was, once we got hunting for these gems, I became so entranced by the mushrooms that I relaxed about where we were. We made a campfire, gathered some wild herbs, and used an empty beer can to cook up some of the most delicious mushrooms I've ever had. Truly simple, wildly tasty.

There are more than 38,000 varieties of mushrooms, not all of them edible. If you want to forage for your own, make sure you have someone knowledgeable with you or you risk making a bad mistake. Foraging at your local market is much less hazardous and almost as rewarding. Each type of mushroom is distinctive and brings its own particular flavour and depth to dishes. Plus mushrooms are highly adaptable.

And remember, mushrooms aren't just for enhancing a dish. They can and should be a dish unto themselves. Mushrooms have a strange and almost alien beauty and exotic taste. Honestly, to me, they're just a wonderment. I can't get enough of them.

CREAM OF MUSHROOM SOUP

If the truffle is king in the mushroom world, then the maitake mushroom is emperor. Delicately battered maitakes and truffled sour cream make for a decadent recipe to be sure. Bringing these two powerhouses together to garnish one simple bowl of creamy mushroom soup makes for a dish that is as radiant as it is sublime.

Serves 4 to 6

For the Soup

¼ cup (60 mL) sour cream
2 tbsp (30 mL) finely chopped chives
1 tsp (5 mL) truffle paste (optional)
Salt and pepper
¼ cup (60 mL) unsalted butter
1 onion, finely chopped
4 shallots, thinly sliced
2 cloves garlic, minced
4 cups (1 L) assorted wild mushrooms, chopped
2 tsp (10 mL) chopped thyme
¼ cup (60 mL) Madeira
4 cups (1 L) vegetable stock (page 247)

For the Maitake Fritters

1 cup (250 mL) all-purpose flour
1 large egg yolk
3 cups (750 mL) vegetable oil
½ lb (250 g) maitake mushrooms
Sea salt

Make the garnish for the soup. Whisk the sour cream with the chives, truffle paste, and salt and pepper to taste. Set aside.

To make the soup, in a large pot over medium heat, melt the butter. Add the onions, shallots, and garlic; cook for 5 minutes, stirring often. Add the mushrooms and thyme; cook for another 5 minutes, stirring often. Add the Madeira and cook until the liquid is reduced by half. Add the stock and bring to a boil, then reduce heat and simmer for 15 minutes. Season with salt and pepper. Working in batches, purée the soup in a blender until smooth and creamy. Return to the pot and keep warm.

To make the fritters, in a bowl, combine 1 cup (250 mL) cold water with 1 cup (250 mL) ice; let sit for 5 minutes. Measure out 1 cup (250 mL) ice water. Using a fork, stir the flour and egg yolk into the ice water until the batter is smooth. In a large, heavy pot, heat the oil over medium-high heat. Working in small batches, dip the mushrooms into the batter and then carefully drop into the hot oil. Fry until the fritters are golden brown. Using a slotted spoon, transfer the fritters to paper towels. Season with sea salt.

To serve, pour the soup into bowls. Spoon some of the truffle sour cream onto each serving and top with the maitake fritters.

POTATOES

You can find a potato of one kind or another growing all over the world, from Ireland to Maine to P.E.I. to Idaho to Alberta—yeah, that's right, Alberta. It was in Strathmore, Alberta, that I found some of the finest and sweetest potatoes I've ever had. Poplar Bluffs Organics grows as many as ten varieties at any one time, and man, are they ever good! And it's all because of the fabulous location. The warm days and cool nights of the Alberta plains are prime conditions for growing sweet, tasty potatoes.

As with all fruit and vegetables, soil and climate give these potatoes

their signature characteristics. And freshness is the ultimate key to best tasting those flavours. Biting into a potato right out of the soil is a truly sublime experience. Get them before the sugars have broken down into starches and you'll be able to taste the rich hazelnut and cream flavours and still smell the wonderful earthiness.

All potatoes are not created equal. Each type has its own distinctive traits that lend it best to specific uses. The Agria is great for frying or roasting, while the Cherry Red is the ultimate boiling potato for soups, stews, or salads. The Russian Blue, so rich in colour and firm in texture, is potato royalty. The bottom line is to think ahead: pick the right potato for the right dish and the potato will be your best friend.

POTATO, DILL, & CHEDDAR SOUP

Soup's on! I have made this potato soup recipe for as long as I can remember! It is creamy, rich, and satisfying. The sharp Cheddar and dill really make this chowder-style soup magic.

Serves 4

¼ cup (60 mL) unsalted butter
2 carrots, cut into ½-inch (1 cm) pieces
2 celery stalks, cut into ½-inch (1 cm) pieces
1 large onion, coarsely chopped
1 leek, cut into ½-inch (1 cm) dice
1½ lb (¾ kg) russet potatoes, peeled and
    cut into ½-inch (1 cm) pieces
Salt and pepper
4 cups (1 L) chicken stock (page 245)
1 cup (250 mL) heavy cream
2 tbsp (30 mL) chopped dill
1 cup (250 mL) grated Cheddar cheese

In a heavy-bottomed pot over medium-high heat, melt the butter. Add the carrots, celery, onion, leek, and potatoes, and season with salt and pepper. Cook until the vegetables begin to brown, about 12 to 15 minutes, stirring occasionally. Add chicken stock, reduce the heat, and simmer, covered, until the vegetables are tender, about 10 minutes. Transfer 3 cups of the soup to a blender, add the cream, and blend until smooth (use caution when blending hot liquids). Return to the pot, and stir in the dill and cheese. Season with salt and pepper to taste.

POTATO & ONION MELT

I like to grow loads of basil in the summer. I harvest it and turn it into fresh, bright green pesto. I freeze it in batches so I have it all year round. It brings dramatic flavour to this unctuous, unfussy gratin recipe that's a breeze to assemble and pop in the oven. The end result is ooey gooey good, better than nachos!

Serves 4

4 large Norland or other baking potatoes, cut into ¼-inch (5 mm) slices
1 leek (white and pale green parts only), thinly sliced
1 small red onion, thinly sliced
6 tbsp (90 mL) olive oil
Leaves from 2 sprigs thyme, chopped
Leaves from 2 sprigs rosemary, chopped
Salt and pepper
4 oz (125 g) Taleggio cheese, sliced
1 small bunch green onions, thinly sliced
½ cup (125 mL) grated Parmesan cheese
¼ cup (60 mL) Basil Pesto (page 253)

Preheat your oven to 350°F (180°C). Line a baking sheet with parchment paper. In a large bowl, toss the potatoes, leeks, and onions with the olive oil, thyme, and rosemary. Season well with salt and pepper. Spread out on the baking sheet and roast until the potatoes are tender, 15 to 20 minutes. Cover with the Taleggio slices. Return to oven and roast for 5 minutes, or until the cheese melts. Remove from oven and sprinkle with the green onions, Parmesan, and pesto.

POTATO-CRUSTED HALIBUT

This is one of my signature dishes. The potato coins on the plump halibut mimic the scales of the fish as it floats on a crest of delicate potato purée. The fresh chive and dill in the deconstructed vichyssoise makes the whole plate light and summery.

Serves 4

For the Potato-Crusted Halibut

2 large Agria or Yukon Gold potatoes, peeled

2 tbsp (30 mL) unsalted butter, melted

4 halibut fillets (each 6 oz/175 g), skinned

Salt and pepper

2 tbsp (30 mL) olive oil

For the Potato Purée

2 lb (1 kg) Agria or Yukon Gold potatoes

6 tbsp (90 mL) unsalted butter

1 cup (250 mL) whole milk, heated

Salt and pepper

For the Vichyssoise Sauce

2 tbsp (30 mL) unsalted butter

1 tbsp (15 mL) olive oil

3 leeks (white and pale green parts only), cut into ½-inch (1 cm) pieces

2 shallots, finely chopped

2 cups (500 mL) peeled Agria or Yukon Gold potatoes cut into ½-inch (1 cm) cubes

1 cup (250 mL) chicken stock (page 245)

1 cup (250 mL) heavy cream

2 tbsp (30 mL) chopped chives

1 tbsp (15 mL) chopped dill

Salt and pepper

To start the potato-crusted halibut, using a mandoline, slice 1 potato into paper-thin rounds. Stack a layer of rounds, and using a 1-inch (2.5 cm) cookie cutter, stamp out potato coins. Lay a piece of plastic wrap on your counter. Arrange potato coins in overlapping even lines on the plastic, pressing them together as you go. Repeat until you have a 4- × 6-inch (10 × 15 cm) layer of potato coins. Brush the potatoes with some of the melted butter. Season a halibut fillet with salt and pepper. Lay the halibut fillet on top of the potatoes, then tightly wrap the fish up in the plastic wrap to press the potatoes to the fish. Refrigerate the fish while preparing the remaining fillets. Refrigerate the fillets for at least 1 hour before cooking.

Meanwhile, begin the potato purée. In a large pot, cover the potatoes with cold salted water. Bring to a boil, then cook over medium heat until a knife inserted into a potato comes away easily, about 30 minutes.

While the potatoes are cooking, make the Vichyssoise sauce. Heat the butter and olive oil in a large saucepan over medium-low heat. Add the leeks and shallots; cook, stirring occasionally, until very soft, about 10 minutes. Add the potatoes and stock. Bring to a boil, then reduce heat to a gentle simmer. Cook until the potatoes are very tender, about 30 minutes. Using a slotted spoon, remove half of the vegetables; set aside and keep warm. Put the remaining mixture in a blender, add the cream, and blend until smooth. Pour into a small saucepan. Add the chives, dill, and salt and pepper to taste. Keep the sauce warm.

To finish the potato purée, drain the potatoes and peel them while still hot. Pass them through a ricer into a heavy saucepan. Stir with a wooden spoon over low heat until steam no longer escapes, about 5 minutes. Add the butter a tablespoon at a time, stirring vigorously until each spoon of butter is melted and thoroughly incorporated. The potatoes should be light and fluffy. Add the milk in a slow stream, beating vigorously to incorporate air into the potatoes. Season with salt and pepper. Keep warm.

To cook the fish, heat the olive oil in a large nonstick skillet over medium-high heat. Use additional oil if needed to generously cover the bottom. Remove the fish from the plastic wrap and place the fish potato side down in the pan. Cook until the potatoes are crispy golden brown, 3 to 4 minutes. Carefully turn the fish and cook for 2 to 3 minutes more or until cooked all the way through.

To serve, place a large spoonful of the potato purée in the centre of each dinner plate. Spoon the reserved vegetables around the purée. Top with the potato-crusted halibut. Spoon the Vichyssoise sauce over the vegetables.

MUSHROOM-STUFFED ONIONS

I love the combination of meaty, roasted mushrooms and sweet, caramelized onions. In this recipe Vidalia onions are stuffed with a mixture of wild mushrooms. I like to use as many different varieties of mushrooms as I can. Try chanterelles, lobster mushrooms, hen of the woods, and black trumpets. They have such wonderful earthy flavours and make for an unbeatable vegetarian dish. Except I put bacon in it!

Serves 4

2 large Vidalia onions, peeled and cut in half crosswise
2 sprigs thyme
2 cups (500 mL) vegetable stock (page 247)
4 tbsp (60 mL) unsalted butter
4 slices bacon, cut into lardons
1 clove garlic, finely chopped
1 lb (500 g) mushrooms, diced
¼ cup (60 mL) white wine
1 cup (250 mL) cherry tomatoes, cut in half
2 tbsp (30 mL) chopped parsley
Salt and pepper
Shaved Parmesan cheese, for garnish

Preheat your oven to 350°F (180°C). Place the onion halves and thyme sprigs in a 2-inch (5 cm) deep baking dish just large enough to hold the onions. Pour the vegetable stock over the onions and dot with half of the butter. Bake for 30 minutes. Remove from oven and let cool. Scoop out the centre of the onions and roughly chop; set aside onion shells and chopped onion.

In a large sauté pan over medium-high heat, cook the bacon until crisp, about 5 minutes. Using a slotted spoon, remove the bacon; set aside. Add the garlic and mushrooms to the pan and cook, stirring often, until the mushrooms are golden brown, about 5 minutes. Deglaze the pan with the wine and reduce the liquid by half. Reduce heat to low and stir in the chopped onions, bacon, tomatoes, parsley, and remaining butter. Cook until the tomatoes are warm and the butter has melted. Remove from heat and season with salt and pepper.

To serve, fill the onion shells with the mushroom mixture and garnish with shaved Parmesan.

TOMATOES

If you've never eaten an heirloom tomato, you're missing out on what a tomato *should* taste like—an explosion of juicy, fresh flavour. When I have to buy commercial tomatoes, my rule of thumb is, if the tomato isn't perfect, don't use it. With heirloom tomatoes, the miraculous thing is that every single tomato is perfect.

Loving these precious tomatoes as I do, I travelled to Homestead, Florida, to visit Tina Borek and her son Mike at their farm to find the finest and freshest heirloom tomatoes of all. I wanted to prepare them a beautiful meal at the end of my stay and found out that, believe it or not, Mike doesn't eat tomatoes. And to boot, Tina's a vegan! This made preparing a meal for these two quite a challenge, but also an exciting chance to turn those restrictions into an opportunity to explore and come up with some interesting and, if I do say so, fantastic dishes. What I find with vegetarian cooking is that you need to do two things: be sure that the meal is complete—that it's not structured around a missing meat—and forget that you're cooking vegetarian.

With ripe, fresh heirloom tomatoes at the heart of a dish, from appetizer to dessert, you can't go wrong. Just ask Mike and Tina.

FRIED GREEN TOMATOES

This southern classic is one of my favourite ways to use end-of-season tomatoes. Served with creamy basil aïoli, these tomatoes are great in a B.L.T.!

Serves 4

4 green tomatoes, sliced ¼ inch (5 mm) thick
Salt and pepper
¾ cup (175 mL) all-purpose flour
¾ cup (175 mL) buttermilk
¼ tsp (1 mL) hot pepper sauce

1½ cups (375 mL) panko bread crumbs
¾ cup (175 mL) yellow cornmeal
Vegetable oil for frying
½ cup (125 mL) Basil Mayonnaise (page 250)

Season the tomatoes with salt and pepper. Place the flour in a shallow dish. In a second shallow dish, whisk together the buttermilk and hot sauce. In a third dish, whisk together the bread crumbs and cornmeal. Working with one slice of tomato at a time, coat the tomato first in flour, then in the buttermilk, and finally in the cornmeal mixture. Lay the tomatoes on a plate, without touching each other. Repeat with the remaining slices.

Add enough oil to a large skillet to coat the bottom. Heat over medium-high heat. Working in batches, fry the tomato slices until golden brown, about 2 minutes per side. Drain on paper towels. Serve the tomatoes warm with the basil mayonnaise.

For the Tomato Tarte Tatin
3 pints (1.5 L) cherry tomatoes, cut in
    half
3 tbsp (50 mL) unsalted butter, softened
4 tsp (20 mL) sugar
8 sun-dried tomatoes, finely chopped
½ lb (250 g) frozen puff pastry dough,
    thawed

For the Thyme Whipped Goat Cheese
4 oz (125 g) soft goat cheese
2 tbsp (30 mL) heavy cream
1 tsp (5 mL) chopped thyme
Salt and pepper

TOMATO TARTE TATIN

This is a delicious twist on the classic French dessert. I like to make this savoury tomato version for cocktail parties or as a starter for Sunday brunch.

Makes 12 tarts

To make the tarte tatin, preheat your oven to 350°F (180°C). Give the cherry tomatoes a squeeze to remove the seeds. Divide the butter among the cups of a muffin pan. Sprinkle the cups with the sugar. Divide half the cherry tomatoes among the muffin cups, top with a layer of sun-dried tomatoes, and then top with the remaining cherry tomatoes. Cover loosely with foil and bake for 30 minutes.

Remove the tomatoes from the oven. Increase the oven temperature to 425°F (220°C). Gently press down on the tomatoes, moulding them to the shape of the cups. On a lightly floured surface, roll out the pastry to a thickness of ⅛ inch (3 mm). Cut out circles large enough to cover the tomatoes in each cup, and poke them all over with a fork. Top each cup with a pastry circle, pressing to seal. Bake for 10 to 15 minutes, until golden brown. Remove from oven and let cool for 15 minutes.

Meanwhile, make the whipped goat cheese. In a food processor, combine the goat cheese, cream, and thyme. Pulse until smooth. Season with salt and pepper.

To serve, run a small knife around the rim of each tart and invert the tarts onto a plate. Top each tart with a small spoonful of the thyme whipped goat cheese.

TOMATO & GOAT CHEESE QUICHE

The reason more people don't make quiche at home is because they're afraid to make the dough for the crust. It can be daunting, but you need fear no more. Frozen puff pastry from the store is a delicious product that can cut down on your prep time incredibly. Just thaw it the night before and putting this whole dish together will only take a few minutes, giving you more time with your brunch guests and your mimosa!

Serves 4 to 6

1 sheet frozen puff pastry dough, thawed
2 branches of cherry tomatoes
on the vine
2 tbsp (30 mL) extra-virgin olive oil
1 clove garlic, minced
1 tsp (5 mL) sugar

1 tsp (5 mL) thyme leaves
Salt and pepper
4 large eggs
½ cup (125 mL) heavy cream
2 tbsp (30 mL) oregano leaves
8 oz (250 g) soft goat cheese

On a lightly floured surface, roll out the pastry large enough to line the bottom and sides of an 11- × 5-inch (28 × 12 cm) tart pan with removable bottom or an 11-inch (28 cm) quiche dish. Gently press the pastry into the pan and trim the edges. Line the pastry with parchment paper and fill with pie weights or dried beans. Chill for at least 20 minutes. Meanwhile, preheat your oven to 350°F (180°C). Bake the tart shell for 20 minutes. Remove the parchment and weights, return the tart shell to the oven, and bake until the pastry is golden, 5 to 10 minutes more. Set aside.

Increase the oven temperature to 400°F (200°C). On a small baking sheet, drizzle the tomatoes on the vine with the olive oil. Sprinkle with the garlic, sugar, thyme, and salt and pepper to taste. Roast until the tomatoes are slightly blistered, about 20 minutes. Remove from oven let cool to room temperature while you make the custard.

Whisk together the eggs, cream, and oregano. Season with salt and pepper. Break the goat cheese into pieces and scatter over the tart shell. Carefully remove the tomatoes from the stems and lay the tomatoes in the tart shell. Pour the egg mixture over the cheese and tomatoes.

Lower the oven temperature to 325°F (160°C). Bake the quiche until the filling is set and the top is golden brown, about 30 minutes. Remove from oven and leave to cool for 5 minutes. Trim the edges if desired, remove the quiche from the pan, and cut into portions.

BURRATA CROSTINI WITH TOMATO CHUTNEY

Creamy burrata, one of my all time favourite cheeses, is incredible with bread still warm from the grill and topped with this delicious, easy-to-prepare chutney. I first discovered white balsamic vinegar while travelling through Italy; it adds a touch of sweetness and depth of flavour to the chutney, perfect for a garden party canapé.

Serves 4

For the Sweet-and-Sour Tomato Chutney
4 cups (1 L) cherry tomatoes
Leaves from 2 sprigs oregano
2 cloves garlic, thinly sliced
Grated zest of 1 lemon
½ cup (125 mL) honey
½ cup (125 mL) white balsamic vinegar
1½ tsp (7 mL) mustard seeds
1 tsp (5 mL) salt
¼ tsp (1 mL) chili flakes
1 vanilla bean, split

For the Burrata
1 clove garlic, peeled
4 slices rustic bread (each about ¾-inch/2 cm thick)
2 tbsp (30 mL) extra-virgin olive oil
8 oz (250 g) burrata
¼ cup (60 mL) toasted pine nuts
4 basil leaves, torn
Sea salt and pepper

Make the sweet-and-sour tomato chutney at least one day ahead so it has plenty of time to marinate. Put the tomatoes and oregano in a large bowl. In a large saucepan, combine the remaining chutney ingredients; stir together with a wooden spoon. Bring to a boil, stirring occasionally, then reduce heat and simmer, stirring occasionally, for 10 minutes. Remove from heat and pour over the tomatoes and oregano. Stir to combine. Cool to room temperature, then cover and marinate overnight in the refrigerator.

To serve the crostini, gently crush the garlic clove and rub over one side of each of the bread slices. Brush both sides of the bread with olive oil. Toast the bread on a grill or in a skillet over medium-high heat until golden and crisp on both sides. Transfer to a platter. Break the burrata roughly with your hands and divide it among the toast slices. Spoon some of the tomato chutney over the cheese and garnish with the pine nuts and basil. Sprinkle with sea salt and pepper.

Here's an idea: You can substitute mozzarella or a soft cheese like a Brie or Camembert.

HEIRLOOM TOMATO FETTUCCINE

Making pasta at home is a great way to remind us that good food doesn't need more than three or four ingredients. You can substitute industrial tomatoes here but don't expect much of a reaction. Heirloom tomatoes are bursting with flavour, so seek them out and your tastebuds will thank you.

Serves 4

4 tbsp (60 mL) olive oil
1 onion, chopped
2 cloves garlic, finely chopped
4 cups (1 L) coarsely chopped yellow heirloom tomatoes
Salt and pepper
14 oz (420 g) dry or 20 oz (600 g) fresh tomato fettucine (page 93)
2 cups (500 mL) red heirloom tomatoes cut into 1-inch (2.5 cm) cubes
½ cup (125 mL) pitted Kalamata olives
2 tbsp (30 mL) capers, drained and chopped
2 cups (500 mL) roughly chopped arugula
¾ cup (175 mL) finely chopped basil
Grated Parmesan cheese for garnish

In a medium saucepan over medium-high heat, heat half the olive oil. Add the onions and garlic; cook, stirring often, until translucent. Add the yellow tomatoes and continue to cook for 20 minutes or until most of the liquid from the tomatoes is reduced. Remove from heat. Using a hand blender, blend the sauce until smooth. Season with salt and pepper. Keep sauce warm.

In a large pot of boiling salted water, cook the fettuccine until al dente, 4 to 5 minutes. Drain the pasta and add it to the sauce. Toss well, and keep warm.

In a large saucepan over medium-high heat, heat the remaining olive oil. Add the red tomatoes, olives, and capers. Cook together until the tomatoes have softened. Add the arugula and basil. Toss together well. Season with salt and pepper.

To serve, divide the pasta among 4 pasta bowls, then top with the tomato and arugula mixture. Garnish with lots of grated Parmesan.

Here's an idea: If you are short on time, buy dry or fresh pasta. If you have time and want something really special, make your own pasta from scratch.

4 cups (1 L) all-purpose flour
2 eggs
6 egg yolks
2 tbsp (30 mL) tomato paste
2 tbsp (30 mL) olive oil
Salt and pepper

Mound the flour on a work surface and make a well in the centre. Add the eggs, egg yolks, tomato paste, oil, salt, and pepper to the well. Using a fork or your fingertips, mix together the egg-tomato mixture, then begin slowly incorporating the flour from the sides. Keep working in the flour until all the flour is incorporated into the dough. Knead for 5 to 10 minutes, until the dough is smooth and elastic. Wrap the dough in plastic wrap and let rest for an hour.

Divide the dough into 4 pieces. Using a hand-cranked pasta machine, roll out the dough into sheets, starting with the widest setting. Lightly flour the dough if it becomes too sticky. Continue to roll the dough, decreasing the size of the setting, until you have the desired thickness of pasta. Cut the sheets into fettuccine noodles. Let them rest in the fridge before cooking.

HOMEMADE TOMATO PASTA

Pasta made from scratch just tastes better and is well worth the extra effort. Simply heaven!

Serves 4

PAN-FRIED COD SALAD

I found many unique ingredients and recipes in Newfoundland, like the cloudberries used here in the vinaigrette. Traditionally these delicate berries are only used in jams and jellies, but I wanted to explore the full range of this ingredient's potential. Scruncheons are salt pork fat, cubed and fried, while a touton is fried bread that is cooked in the scruncheon fat.

Serves 4

For the Touton Croutons
1 tsp (5 mL) sugar
1 cup (250 mL) lukewarm water
1½ tsp (7 mL) instant yeast
2 cups (500 mL) flour
1 tsp (5 mL) salt
¼ cup (60 mL) scruncheons or bacon cut into ¼-inch (5 mm) dice

For the Cod
4 cod fillets (each 4 oz/125 g)
Salt and pepper
Flour for dredging
2 tbsp (30 mL) canola oil
3 tbsp (50 mL) unsalted butter

For the Salad
4 cups (1 L) chopped romaine lettuce
1 cucumber, thinly sliced
5 radishes, thinly sliced
1 bunch parsley, chopped
½ cup (125 mL) Balsamic Cloudberry Vinaigrette (page 257)

To make the touton croutons, in a large bowl dissolve the sugar in the lukewarm water. Sprinkle with the yeast and let stand until foamy, about 10 minutes. Add half of the flour and the salt; stir until smooth. Gradually add more flour, a spoonful at a time, until the dough no longer sticks to the bowl. Turn the dough out onto a lightly floured surface and knead for at least 10 minutes, until the dough is smooth and elastic. Shape into a ball. Lightly oil a large bowl with olive oil and place the dough in it, turning to coat with oil. Cover with a damp cloth and let rise in a warm place until the dough has doubled in size, about 1½ hours. Punch down the dough and divide into quarters. On a lightly floured surface, roll each quarter into a circle ½ inch (1 cm) thick.

In a medium skillet over medium heat, cook the scruncheons until crispy. Using a slotted spoon, remove them from the pan and drain on paper towels; set aside for the salad. Working with one dough circle at a time, fry the toutons in the scruncheon fat, turning once, until golden, 3 to 5 minutes per side. Transfer toutons to a plate. Cut into wedges.

To cook the cod, heat a large skillet over medium-high heat. Season the fish with salt and pepper. Lightly dredge the fish in the flour and shake off any excess. Add the oil and butter to the pan. When the butter has melted, add the fish and cook, without disturbing, until a golden crust forms, about 3 minutes. Turn the fish and continue to cook for about 2 minutes or until the fish is cooked through and golden on the bottom. Remove from the pan and keep warm.

To make the salad, in a large bowl, toss together the romaine, cucumber, radishes, and parsley. Dress the salad with the vinaigrette and toss again.

To serve, divide the salad among 4 plates. Top with the pan-fried cod and the crispy scruncheons. Garnish with a few fried touton wedges.

For the Venison

Leaves from 2 sprigs fresh thyme
5 dried juniper berries
Salt and pepper
4 tbsp (60 mL) olive oil
1 venison loin (2 lb/1 kg), trimmed
4 shallots, thinly sliced
1 clove garlic, thinly sliced
1 sprig thyme
1 cup (250 mL) red wine
¼ cup (60 mL) unsalted butter, cut into
    1-inch (2.5 cm) pieces
Cloudberry Chutney (page 99)

For the Sweet Potato Gratin

2 tbsp (30 mL) unsalted butter
2 sweet potatoes, peeled and thinly
    sliced
2 shallots, sliced
2 tbsp (30 mL) chopped thyme
Salt and pepper
1 cup (250 mL) grated Gruyère cheese
1½ cups (375 mL) heavy cream

VENISON WITH SWEET POTATO GRATIN

This was another chance for me to explore new ways to use Newfoundland's favourite berry, the cloudberry. What goes better with rich, dark venison than a fruity chutney, scented with warm cider vinegar and woody herbs? If you said "nothing," you are absolutely correct. Sided with a sweet potato gratin oozing with Gruyère, here is a plate inspired by the wilds of Newfoundland.

Serves 4

To ready the venison, in a mortar and pestle, grind the thyme and juniper berries with a pinch of salt and pepper. Transfer to a large bowl and add half of the olive oil; stir together. Add the venison and turn to coat well with the oil. Marinate the venison in the oil, covered and refrigerated, for 1 to 2 hours.

While the venison is marinating, and about an hour before serving, make the sweet potato gratin. Preheat your oven to 375°F (190°C). Line a 9-inch (23 cm) square baking pan with parchment paper and rub the butter over the bottom and sides. Make a layer of sweet potatoes, slightly overlapping. Sprinkle with some of the shallots, thyme, salt and pepper, and Gruyère. Repeat, ending with the rest of the Gruyère. Pour over the cream and cover with foil. Bake for 50 minutes to 1 hour or until a knife slides through the potatoes easily. Set aside and keep warm. Slice into portions when you are ready to serve.

To finish the venison, in a large skillet over medium-high heat, sear the meat on all sides, 8 to 10 minutes for medium doneness. Transfer to a plate and let rest, covered loosely with foil. Reduce heat to medium. Add the remaining olive oil to the skillet. Add the shallots and garlic. Cook, stirring, until translucent and tender. Turn up the heat, add the thyme and wine, and reduce the wine by half. Reduce heat and simmer gently for 4 minutes. Remove the pan from the heat, add the butter, a piece at a time, swirling the pan around to melt and incorporate the butter into the sauce. Season to taste.

To serve, slice the venison into thick slices and arrange on plates. Spoon over some pan sauce and garnish with cloudberry chutney. Serve with the sweet potato gratin.

Here's an idea: You can substitute blackberries or cranberries for the cloudberries.

CLOUDBERRIES (BAKEAPPLES)

A visit to the Rock should be on everybody's agenda. If you don't go for the fish or the scenery or the warmth and hospitality of the people, then for heaven's sake, go for the cloudberries. Like Newfoundland itself, the cloudberry is a wild and wonderful thing of beauty. Also known as bakeapples, they're a close relative of the raspberry.

This elusive berry has a very short season, so you can get cloudberries fresh in Newfoundland only for a small window each year. This makes it even more of a treasure, especially in today's world of never-out-of-season foods.

The cloudberry smells both musky and pineapple-sweet, has a mild crunch, and is on the tart side. These rare and unique berries grow near bogs and on cliff sides, and are prized partly because they're hard to come by. I risked my neck getting them, that's for sure, but come on. You only live once, right? Getting some cloudberry jam, which you can find at specialty shops or online, and spreading it on some sweet scones is a great way to experience the cloudberry if you can't get down East to harvest some for yourself.

2 tbsp (30 mL) olive oil
1 onion, thinly sliced
2 cloves garlic, minced
½ tsp (2 mL) chili flakes
¼ cup (60 mL) sherry vinegar
¼ cup (60 mL) honey
1 tbsp (15 mL) Dijon mustard
1 cup (250 mL) cloudberries
1 tsp (5 mL) chopped thyme
Salt and black pepper

Heat the oil in a large skillet over medium-high heat. Add the onions and garlic. Cook, stirring often, until the onions are golden brown. Stir in the chili flakes, vinegar, honey, and mustard; cook for 2 minutes. Reduce heat to medium and add the cloudberries and thyme. Cook, stirring occasionally, until the cloudberries start to break down and the chutney has the consistency of a thick sauce, another 20 to 30 minutes. Season with salt and pepper.

CLOUD-BERRY CHUTNEY

These delicate berries grown in the bogs around Newfoundland are a delicacy. When ripe they are a gorgeous golden amber colour and are soft and juicy with a distinctive tart taste. They are mostly made into sweet jams, tarts, and syrups. I wanted to capture their unique taste in a savoury chutney, which becomes a perfect condiment for game and meats.

Makes 1½ cups (375 mL)

CRANBERRIES

East Freetown, Massachusetts, is a place of exquisite northeastern-style beauty. When I got there, bright red cranberry bogs dotted the whole of the picturesque landscape. Seeing that gorgeous vista, I was inspired to use cranberries to prepare an autumn extravaganza because, for me, nothing says fall like fresh cranberries.

When I arrived, I was met by Stefan Ashley, alias Cranberry Santa—a bushy-white-bearded, third-generation cranberry farmer who, along with his daughter-in-law, two grandkids, and son, runs the family cranberry farm. This kind of place is getting rarer all the time—a real family farm business, passed down from generation to generation.

Stefan says the first cranberry always bites back. When raw, a cranberry crunches like an apple and sends shivers of tart delight bursting into your mouth. Picking cranberries is backbreaking work, but the results are delicious berries with more flavour than any other you can eat. Their tartness combines wonderfully with rich, fatty foods like duck and pork, cutting the heaviness of the meat with their intense fruitiness.

Even if you can't get them from Cran-San himself, fresh cranberries are a versatile and delicious way to bring berries to the fall table.

BACON-WRAPPED DUCK WITH CRAN-BERRIES

A succulent duck breast stuffed with bright green spinach and studded with ruby red cranberries would be a welcome sight on any dinner plate. But I just wasn't satisfied; I knew this duck could do better, so I did the best thing you can do in a situation like this and wrapped the whole thing in bacon.

Serves 4

2 tbsp (30 mL) olive oil
2 onions, quartered lengthwise
2 tbsp (30 mL) unsalted butter
Salt and pepper
1 cup (250 mL) chicken stock (page 245)
12 thin slices bacon
2 boneless skinless duck breasts, butterflied
1 cup (250 mL) cooked spinach
¼ cup (60 mL) sun-dried cranberries

Preheat your oven to 375°F (190°C). In an ovenproof saucepan, heat 1 tbsp (15 mL) of the olive oil over medium-high heat. Carefully place the onions in the pan cut side down. Cook until golden brown, about 2 minutes on each side. Add the butter and cook the onions in the foaming butter for 4 minutes. Season with salt and pepper. Add the chicken stock. Transfer the pan to the oven and bake until the onions are soft, 20 to 25 minutes. Let cool, then separate into petals.

Place 6 slices of bacon lengthwise on a work surface, overlapping them slightly. Place a duck breast in the centre. Season the duck with salt and pepper.

Arrange half of the spinach in a thin layer along the centre of the breast. Top with a row of onion petals, then sprinkle with half the cranberries. Fold the duck over onto itself to form a roll. Fold the bacon over the duck, and then roll it up to make a neat package. Tie the duck breast at intervals with butcher's twine. Repeat with the remaining duck breast.

In a large ovenproof skillet, heat the remaining olive oil over medium heat. Carefully place the bacon-wrapped duck breast in the pan and cook all sides for about 6 minutes, until the bacon is browned. Drain off most of the fat. Transfer the pan to the oven to finish the cooking, 15 to 20 minutes. Transfer the duck to a cutting board and let rest for 5 to 8 minutes. Cut each duck breast into thick slices.

IN THE ORCHARD

AVOCADOS

De Luz, California, is where JC Iamurri of Avocado Express grows the best of the best. JC's avocado groves feature different varieties, including Hass, the pear-shaped kind you normally find in grocery stores, and Reeds, the buttery globes about the size of a baseball, and they taste like heaven.

I couldn't help falling in love with avocado oil. This emerald-green oil is silky and rich, with a naturally sweet, slightly nutty flavour. What puts avocado oil over the top is its high smoke point (you can use it to fry ingredients to incredible crispness).

Avocado can be sweet for salads and out of this world for desserts too. You can make it the star of a meal. Don't be afraid to cook it, grill it, or tempura-fry it.

GUACAMOLE

This avocado dip is one of my most favourite snacks. The fresh lime and cilantro brighten the taste, but it's the avocado oil that gives it such an incredible rich avocado flavour. So delicious, healthy, and easy to make.
Makes 2 cups (500 mL)

6 tbsp (90 mL) finely diced red onion
2 tbsp (30 mL) lime juice
2 avocados
1 tomato, chopped
1 tsp (5 mL) minced seeded jalapeño pepper
2 tbsp (30 mL) chopped cilantro
Salt and pepper

In a medium bowl, combine the onions and lime juice. Let stand for 5 minutes. Halve the avocados and, using a spoon, scoop the flesh into the bowl. Add the tomato, jalapeño, and cilantro; stir together. Season with salt and pepper.

SHRIMP WITH SALSA & AVOCADO

Get everyone in the kitchen to make this fun recipe by mashing avocado, juicing lime for the salsa, and cleaning the shrimp. These gorgeous little prosciutto-wrapped appetizers are fantastic on the barbecue where they will grill up tender and juicy.

Serves 4

For the Prosciutto-Wrapped Shrimp
3 tbsp (50 mL) avocado oil
1 lime, cut in half
1 clove garlic, minced
1 tsp (5 mL) finely diced jalapeño pepper
Salt and pepper
1 lb (500 g) jumbo shrimp, peeled, deveined, and butterflied
1 avocado
2 tbsp (30 mL) chopped cilantro
¼ lb (125 g) thin slices prosciutto, cut lengthwise into strips 2 inches (5 cm) wide

For the Tomato Salsa
2 cups (500 mL) tomatoes
1 jalapeño pepper, seeded and finely chopped
1 small red onion, finely diced
¼ cup (125 mL) cilantro sprigs, chopped
2 tbsp (30 mL) lime juice
1 tsp (5 mL) minced garlic
1 tsp (5 mL) sugar
Salt and pepper

First, marinate the shrimp. In a medium bowl, whisk together 2 tbsp (30 mL) of the avocado oil, the juice of half a lime, the garlic, jalapeño, and salt to taste. Add the shrimp and toss to coat. Let stand at room temperature for about 20 minutes.

Meanwhile, preheat your grill to medium-high.

While the shrimp are marinating, make the salsa. Dice the tomatoes and transfer to a bowl. Stir in the jalapeño, onion, cilantro, lime juice, garlic, sugar, and salt and pepper to taste. Set aside.

To make the avocado stuffing for the shrimp, scoop the avocado flesh into a bowl and mash with a fork. Stir in the remaining avocado oil, the juice of the remaining half lime, the cilantro, and salt and pepper to taste.

To stuff the shrimp, lay them out flat on a work surface. Spread about 1 tsp (5 mL) of the avocado mixture inside each shrimp. Carefully close the shrimp and wrap a strip of prosciutto around each shrimp. Grill the shrimp until the prosciutto is crispy and the shrimp are opaque and cooked through, about 3 minutes per side.

Serve hot off the grill with the tomato salsa.

TUNA STEAKS WITH SALSA

Everyone loves tuna. I make sure to use only really good quality, sustainable tuna that is Ocean Wise approved; same goes for all the fish I buy. The avocado salsa verde is cool, creamy, and refreshing with a bit of a kick.

Serves 4

4 tuna steaks (each 6 oz/175 g and about 1 inch/2.5 cm thick)

Zest and juice of 1 lemon

1 tbsp (15 mL) thyme leaves

1 tsp (5 mL) sambal oelek

¼ cup (60 mL) plus 2 tbsp (30 mL) avocado oil

2 tbsp (30 mL) finely diced shallots

Salt and pepper

1 avocado

2 tbsp (30 mL) finely chopped capers

2 tbsp (30 mL) roughly chopped mixed pitted olives

1 bunch chives, chopped

¼ cup (60 mL) chopped parsley

¼ cup (60 mL) chopped chervil

Rub the tuna on both sides with the lemon zest, thyme, sambal oelek, and 2 tbsp (30 mL) of the avocado oil. Cover and refrigerate for 2 hours.

In a small bowl, stir together the lemon juice, shallots, and a pinch of salt; let sit for 5 minutes. Peel the avocado and cut into 1-inch (2.5 cm) cubes. Add the avocado to the shallots along with the capers, olives, and remaining ¼ cup (60 mL) avocado oil. Set aside the salsa verde.

Preheat your grill to high heat. Season the tuna with salt and pepper. Grill the tuna, rotating it once or twice to give it grill marks, 2 to 3 minutes per side. The tuna should be well seared but still rare in the middle.

Stir the chives, parsley, and chervil into the salsa verde and season with salt and pepper. Serve the tuna topped with the salsa verde.

PIRI-PIRI FLANK STEAK WITH SALAD & FRITES

When I was in De Luz, California, I got to cook on a state-of-the-art outdoor grill surrounded by palm trees and orchards. I was so excited by the grill that I cooked everything on it. If you're a serious griller this is the dish for you.

Serves 6 to 8

For the Flank Steaks
¼ cup (60 mL) avocado oil
2 tbsp (30 mL) Piri-Piri Spice Rub (page 260)
½ cup (125 mL) chopped cilantro
2 medium flank steaks
Salt and pepper

For the Grilled Vegetable Salad
2 large ears of corn, husked
2 poblano chilies
6 tbsp (90 mL) avocado oil
12 small pattypan squash, cut in half
1 red onion, peeled and cut into ¼-inch (½ cm) slices
2 zucchini, cut lengthwise into slices ⅓ inch (8 mm) thick
1 red bell pepper, cut into quarters and seeded
1 yellow bell pepper, cut into quarters and seeded
1 bunch asparagus
Salt and black pepper
⅓ cup (75 mL) thinly sliced green onions
⅓ cup (75 mL) chopped cilantro
Zest and juice of 2 limes

For the Avocado Frites
About 2 cups (500 mL) avocado oil
¼ cup (60 mL) all-purpose flour
¼ tsp (1 mL) kosher salt, plus more to taste
2 eggs, beaten
1¼ cups (300 mL) panko bread crumbs
2 avocados
Avocado Aïoli (page 251)

To prepare the flank steaks, in a baking dish large enough to hold the steaks, combine the avocado oil, piri-piri spice rub, and cilantro. Add the steaks, turning to coat with the marinade. Cover and refrigerate for 2 hours.

Preheat your grill to high. Remove the steaks from the marinade, taking off excess marinade with paper towel. Season the steaks well with salt and pepper. Grill steaks for 3 to 4 minutes on each side for medium-rare. Transfer to a cutting board and let rest for 5 minutes.

To make the vegetable salad, reduce the grill to medium-high. Brush the corn and poblano chilies with some of the avocado oil. Grill, turning occasionally, until tender and slightly charred, about 10 minutes. When the corn is cool enough to handle, use a small knife to shave off the kernels into a large bowl. Peel the poblano chilies, then remove the stems, seeds, and membranes; coarsely chop and add to the corn. Brush the pattypan squash, onion, zucchini, red and yellow peppers, and asparagus with some of the avocado oil; season with salt and pepper. Grill the vegetables until just cooked. Toss into the corn and poblano mixture. Add the green onions, cilantro, lime zest and juice, and the remaining avocado oil. Season with salt and pepper and toss together well.

To make the avocado frites, preheat your oven to 200°F (100°C). In a medium saucepan, heat 1½ inches (4 cm) of oil to 375°F (190°C). In a shallow dish, combine the flour and the salt. In a second dish, beat the eggs. Put the bread crumbs in a third dish. Peel the avocado and slice the flesh into ½-inch (1 cm) wedges. Dip the wedges in the flour, shaking off excess. Dip in egg, then roll in the bread crumbs to coat. As they're breaded, set them on a small baking sheet in a single layer. Fry one-quarter of the avocado wedges at a time until deep golden, 30 to 60 seconds. Transfer in a single layer to a platter lined with paper towels. Keep warm in the oven while cooking the remaining avocado. Sprinkle with salt to taste.

Slice steak into thin slices and serve with the avocado frites and grilled vegetable, with the avocado aïoli on the side.

LIMES

I travelled to a farm in California to roll up my sleeves and learn about limes. It's always lime time on the farm, since they produce so many different kinds. There are of course Mexican limes, the ones you usually see in the grocery store, and key limes, those small, intense ones that are the central ingredient in wonderful key lime pie. There are Australian finger limes, like citrus caviar, and Palestine

sweet limes, so sweet you can eat both the skin and the flesh—and those are just some of the varieties I tried on the farm. Each one is special and has a unique quality for cooking with.

I'm a big believer in simplicity, but there are occasions when mixing the right combination of foods together, and sometimes introducing the odd couple of ingredients, can make for a truly inspired dish. Limes meet chocolate, or limes and beets, or limes with horseradish. Experiment. Play around. Make magic!

SALMON CEVICHE WITH LIME-MARINATED BEETS

I love ceviche. It is the best way to cook in the summertime since no oven is required. The jewel tones of the cubed beets beside the blushing pink salmon, garnished with a scoop of horseradish lime sour cream, make for a truly beautiful finished dish.

Serves 4

For the Salmon Ceviche

8 oz (250 g) skinless salmon fillet, cut into ½-inch (1 cm) cubes
Zest and juice of 2 limes
1 tsp (5 mL) finely grated fresh horseradish
1 bunch chives, thinly sliced
1 jalapeño pepper, seeded and finely chopped
4 tbsp olive oil
Salt and pepper
1 cup (250 mL) pea greens
2 radishes, julienned

For the Lime-Marinated Beets

6 small red beets, greens removed
4 sprigs thyme
¼ cup (60 mL) kosher salt
¼ cup (60 mL) sherry vinegar
2 tbsp (30 mL) sugar
Zest and juice of 1 lime
¼ cup (60 mL) olive oil
Salt and pepper

For the Horseradish Lime Sour Cream

⅓ cup (75 mL) sour cream
2 tsp (10 mL) finely grated fresh horseradish
1 tbsp (15 mL) finely chopped chives
1 tbsp (15 mL) lime juice
Salt

In a large bowl, combine the salmon, lime zest and juice, horseradish, chives, jalapeño, and olive oil. Season well with salt and pepper. Cover and refrigerate for 1 to 2 hours.

Meanwhile, make the lime-marinated beets. In a saucepan combine the beets, thyme, kosher salt, vinegar, and sugar. Cover with water and bring to a boil, then reduce heat and simmer uncovered until the beets are fork-tender, about 1 hour. Drain the beets and run under cold water. Slip off the skin. Dry the beets and cut into ¼-inch (5 mm) dice. Transfer to a bowl. Toss with the lime zest and juice and olive oil; season well with salt and pepper. Cover and let marinate in the refrigerator until ready to serve.

Now you can make the horseradish lime sour cream. In a small bowl, mix all of the ingredients together and season well.

To serve, spoon the salmon onto the centre of 4 salad plates. Place some marinated beets on top of the salmon. Spoon a dollop of the horseradish sour cream on top. Garnish with pea greens and julienned radishes.

SCALLOPS WITH CARROT PURÉE

The sweet honey, bright citrus, and hot red pepper flakes combine to make a delectable glaze for the tender scallops.

Serves 4

For the Gingered Carrot Purée

1 cup (250 mL) peeled carrots cut into
    ½-inch (1 cm) rounds
Zest and juice of 2 oranges
¾ cup (175 mL) water
1 tsp (5 mL) grated ginger
2 tbsp (30 mL) unsalted butter
Salt and pepper

For the Scallops

12 large sea scallops
Salt and pepper
2 tsp (10 mL) unsalted butter
1 tsp (5 mL) olive oil
2 tbsp (30 mL) wildflower honey
Pinch red pepper flakes
Zest and juice of 1 orange

To make the carrot purée, in a medium, heavy saucepan, combine the carrots, orange zest and juice, water, and ginger. Bring to a boil, then reduce heat and simmer until the carrots are very soft, about 30 minutes. Transfer the carrots and the remaining liquid to a blender. Add the butter and blend until smooth. Season with salt and pepper. Keep warm.

To prepare the scallops, pull off the small side muscle, rinse the scallops with cold water, and thoroughly pat dry. Season with salt and pepper.

Heat the butter and olive oil in a large skillet over high heat. Carefully place the scallops in the pan. Sear the scallops, without moving them, for 1½ minutes, then turn the scallops over and cook for another 1 to 2 minutes or until they have a golden crust and are just opaque in the centre. Remove from heat and drizzle the honey, red pepper flakes, orange juice, and zest over the scallops.

To serve, spoon a bed of carrot purée onto 4 plates. Top with 3 scallops per serving.

VEGETABLE BHAJIS

These crispy Indian-spiced vegetable fritters make a perfect snack on their own, but they can be used in so many other ways. They are a great base to make canapés or garnishes for soups and salads. My favourite way to serve them is with my Scallops with Carrot Purée on page 122.

Makes 12 bhajis

½ cup (125 mL) chickpea flour
½ cup (125 mL) all-purpose flour
1 tsp (5 mL) turmeric
½ tsp (2 mL) paprika
¼ tsp (1 mL) ground cumin
1 tsp (5 mL) salt
½ tsp (2 mL) pepper
½ tsp (2 mL) baking powder
1 cup (250 mL) water

2 tbsp (30 mL) olive oil
1 leek, white and pale green parts only, julienned
1 carrot, julienned
2 green onions, thinly sliced diagonally
1 red onion, thinly sliced lengthwise and pieces separated
Sea salt

In a medium bowl, combine the chickpea flour, all-purpose flour, turmeric, paprika, cumin, salt, pepper, and baking powder. Slowly stir in the water. Stir with a wooden spoon to make a bright yellow batter.

Heat the olive oil in a large nonstick skillet over medium-high heat. Working in small batches, drop the vegetables into the batter. Lift them out, letting excess batter drip off, then carefully transfer to the hot oil. Cook until golden brown on both sides. Drain on paper towels and season with sea salt.

Serve them warm on a platter.

SIRLOIN STEAK & POTATO SALAD

Don't be afraid to cook with salt. Besides keeping the meat super moist and wowing your guests, it's also a lot of fun to do. Serve this incredibly tender meat with a delicious warm fingerling potato salad.

Serves 4

For the Salt-Crusted Sirloin Steak
2 New York strip steaks (each 1 lb/500 g)
3 tbsp (50 mL) extra-virgin olive oil
Freshly ground black pepper
6 egg whites
3 cups (750 mL) kosher salt
2 bay leaves
Leaves from 3 sprigs rosemary
Leaves from 4 sprigs thyme
Zest and juice of 4 limes

For the Warm Potato Salad
1 lb (500 g) fingerling potatoes
Juice of 2 limes
¼ cup (60 mL) grated Parmesan cheese
¼ cup (60 mL) olive oil
1 tbsp (15 mL) Dijon mustard
1 clove garlic, minced
2 green onions, thinly sliced
2 tbsp (30 mL) chopped parsley
Salt and pepper

Preheat your oven to 475°F (240°C). Drizzle the steaks with 2 tbsp (30 mL) of the olive oil and season with black pepper. In a large bowl, gently whisk the egg whites until slightly foamy. Add the kosher salt, bay leaves, rosemary, thyme, and lime zest and juice. Combine well until it holds together like wet sand. Set aside.

Heat the remaining olive oil in a large skillet over medium-high heat. Cook the steaks for 1 to 2 minutes on each side or until well seared.

Place the steaks in another large skillet and mould the salt paste on top of and around them to completely enclose them. Bake for 15 minutes (internal temperature should reach 120°F/50°C), then remove from oven and let rest for 7 or 8 minutes.

Meanwhile, cook the potatoes in boiling salted water just until tender. Drain. Allow to cool for about 5 minutes, then cut them in half lengthwise and put in a large bowl. In a small bowl, whisk together the lime juice, Parmesan, olive oil, mustard, garlic, green onions, and parsley. Season well with salt and pepper. Pour the dressing over the potatoes and gently toss to coat. Season well with salt and pepper.

To serve, crack open the salt shell and transfer the steaks to a cutting board. Cut into thick slices. Serve with the warm potato salad.

4 ears of corn, with husks
1 tbsp (15 mL) extra-virgin olive oil
Salt and pepper
½ cup (125 mL) Cilantro Finger Lime Aïoli (page 252)
1 cup (250 mL) queso fresco, crumbled
½ cup (125 mL) chopped cilantro
Ancho chili powder for dusting
2 limes, cut into wedges

Preheat your grill to medium-high. Peel back the husks from the corn, leaving them attached at the ends and twisting them to make handles. Remove the silk. Brush each cob with olive oil and season with salt and pepper. Grill the cobs for 15 to 20 minutes, turning often. When fully cooked, transfer them to a plate, slather them with the aïoli, then roll them in the queso fresco. Sprinkle with the cilantro and chili powder and serve with lime wedges.

GRILLED MEXICAN CORN

I discovered finger limes in California. Their pulp is so unique, it's like lime caviar. Try to get your hands on some finger limes for this recipe, no pun intended! Sweet corn grilled over charcoal, then kissed with bright, tart lime aïoli and rolled in queso fresco: What more could you ask for on a sunny summer day, except for an icy cold cerveza?

Serves 4

SHRIMP WITH OLIVE TORTILLAS & BLACK BEANS

In France, they poach shellfish in butter, in California they poach it in olive oil, and either way you get the most succulent, tender meat. Here I've infused the oil with lemon, peppercorns, and thyme. I served these tantalizing shrimp on fresh tortillas studded with Kalamata olives.

Serves 6

For the Lime Sour Cream
1 cup (250 mL) sour cream
Zest and juice of 1 lime
Salt and freshly ground black pepper

For the Tomatillo Avocado Salsa
2 avocados
1 cup (250 mL) diced tomatillos
3 green onions, thinly sliced
1 jalapeño pepper, seeded and
    finely chopped
3 tbsp (50 mL) chopped cilantro
3 tbsp (50 mL) olive oil
1 tbsp (15 mL) lime juice
Salt and pepper

For the Olive-Oil-Poached Shrimp
and Salad
2 cups (500 mL) olive oil
2 shallots, thinly sliced
2 cloves garlic, crushed
3 sprigs thyme
½ tsp (2 mL) black peppercorns
4 slices of lemon
18 large shrimp, peeled and deveined
3 cups (750 mL) baby arugula
1 cup (250 mL) thinly sliced radishes
¼ cup (60 mL) slivered assorted olives
1 cup (250 mL) watercress
3 tbsp (50 mL) olive oil
1 tbsp (15 mL) rice vinegar
Salt and pepper
4 oz (125 g) queso fresco, crumbled
Cilantro sprigs and 6 lime wedges
    for garnish

For the Black Beans
1 tbsp (15 mL) olive oil
½ onion, finely chopped
1 clove garlic, minced
2 tsp (10 mL) ground cumin
½ tsp (2 mL) chili flakes
8 oz (250 g) cooked black beans
¼ cup (60 mL) water
Salt and pepper
½ bunch cilantro, minced

For the Olive Tortillas
(makes 12 tortillas)
2½ cups (625 mL) all-purpose flour
½ cup (125 mL) cold butter,
    cut into pieces
2 tbsp (30 mL) finely chopped
    pitted Kalamata olives
1 tsp (5 mL) salt
1 cup (250 mL) warm water

To make the lime sour cream, combine all the ingredients and mix well. Refrigerate until ready to use.

To make the tomatillo salsa, peel the avocados, dice the flesh, and put in a bowl. Add the rest of the ingredients and mix well. Cover and set aside.

To poach the shrimp, in a medium saucepan over medium-high heat, heat 1 tbsp (15 mL) of the olive oil. Add the shallots and garlic and cook, stirring often, until translucent. Add the thyme, peppercorns, lemon slices, and the rest of the olive oil. Bring to a boil, then remove from heat and let stand for 15 minutes to infuse the flavours. Return oil to medium heat, add the shrimp, and poach just until the shrimp are cooked, 3 to 4 minutes. Remove the shrimp from the oil and let cool.

To prepare the black beans, in a large saucepan over medium heat, add the olive oil, onions, and garlic; cook, stirring often, until translucent. Add the cumin and chili flakes; cook, stirring, for another minute. Add the beans and water; season with salt and pepper. Reduce heat to low and cook, stirring occasionally, for 15 minutes to infuse the flavours. Remove from heat, stir in the cilantro, and season well with salt and pepper.

While the beans are cooking, make the olive tortillas. In the bowl of a mixer, combine the flour, butter, olives, and salt. Beat with the paddle until crumbly, 3 to 5 minutes. Gradually add the warm water and continue mixing until the dough is smooth, about 3 minutes. Divide the dough into 12 pieces. Roll each into a ball and place on a baking sheet; cover with a lint-free towel and let rest for 15 minutes. On a lightly floured surface, roll out each ball into an 8-inch (20 cm) circle. Heat a 12-inch (30 cm) skillet over medium heat. Cook the tortillas, one at a time, until puffy and slightly brown, 30 to 45 seconds per side. Set aside on a platter to cool slightly.

To make the salad, in a large bowl, combine the arugula, radishes, olives, and watercress. Toss with the olive oil and rice vinegar. Season with salt and pepper.

To serve, place a warm tortilla on each plate and top each with a tablespoon (15 mL) of black beans. Place 3 poached shrimp on top of the beans, and top with a small mound of the salad. Top with the salsa and queso fresco. Drizzle with some lime sour cream and garnish with cilantro sprigs and lime.

OLIVES

I'm a huge fan of remarkable California olives. They're plump and fruity, which makes for delicious olive oil too. Excellent olive oil tastes the same as excellent olives smell—fresh, sweet, and tart.

I'm also a huge fan of California wines. While I was travelling out there, I had the opportunity to visit a truly unique winery called New Clairvaux Vineyards that's run by Cistercian monks. They make a Petite Sirah that's out of this world. Like the olive oil from the region, it's fruity and has the perfect balance of acid. Maybe I'm just a big fan of California and most everything it produces.

A highlight of the trip for me was my first chance to smoke beef with olive wood. It worked like a charm. Olive wood gives a light mesquite-style earthiness to the smoke, which balanced perfectly with the fruitiness of the olive oil and the Petite Sirah.

So a lasting memory for me was the dining table shared by a chef, two monks, a winemaker, and three generations of olive farmers. From each of us, a contribution that was a labour of love. And all of us, fans of the others. And definitely fans of zesty olives.

FILET MIGNON & OLIVE OIL MASH

I came up with this recipe on an olive farm in California while I was smoking the tenderloin over olive branches. If you don't happen to have any olive branches kicking around, don't fret. You'll still get intense olive flavour from the hearty olive ragout and the silky olive oil mashed potatoes.

Serves 4

For the Filet Mignon

1 tbsp (15 mL) black peppercorns
1 tbsp (15 mL) white peppercorns
1 tbsp (15 mL) pink peppercorns
Zest of 1 orange
2 tbsp (30 mL) kosher salt
2 tbsp (30 mL) olive oil
4 centre-cut beef tenderloin filets
   (each 6 oz/175 g)
2 sprigs thyme
2 cloves garlic, crushed
3 tbsp (50 mL) unsalted butter
Salt and pepper

For the Roasted Chili and Olive Ragout

1 red bell pepper
1 yellow bell pepper
2 jalapeño peppers
1 poblano chili
4 tbsp (60 mL) olive oil
1 red onion, thinly sliced
½ cup (125 mL) pitted olives, chopped
2 cloves garlic, minced
1 tbsp (15 mL) chopped parsley
Salt and black pepper

For the Olive Oil Mash

2 lb (1 kg) large russet potatoes,
   peeled and quartered
⅓ cup (75 mL) extra-virgin olive oil
¼ cup (60 mL) pitted olives, finely chopped
Salt and pepper

To make the coating for the beef, preheat your oven to 350°F (180°C). Combine all the peppercorns in a dry ovenproof skillet and toast them in the oven for 5 minutes. Coarsely grind into a small bowl. Stir in the orange zest and kosher salt. Set aside.

To make the ragout, increase the oven temperature to 400°F (200°C). Place all the peppers and chili on a baking sheet and toss with 2 tbsp (30 mL) of the olive oil to coat. Roast until the skins are blackened and blistered, about 15 minutes. Transfer to a bowl, cover with plastic wrap, and let cool. Peel off and discard the skins. Seed the peppers and cut them into strips.

In a sauté pan over medium-high heat, heat the remaining olive oil. Add the red onions and cook, stirring occasionally, until the onions are golden brown, about 6 minutes. Stir in the olives, garlic, and pepper and chili strips; continue to cook for 2 minutes. Remove from heat, stir in the parsley, and season with salt and pepper. Set aside, keeping warm.

Meanwhile, make the olive oil mash. Cover the potatoes with cold salted water and bring to a boil. Cook until tender, about 20 minutes. Drain the potatoes, return them to the pot, and mash them. Stir in the olive oil, olives, and salt and pepper to taste. Set aside, keeping warm.

To finish the steaks, preheat your oven to 350°F (180°C). Heat the olive oil in a heavy skillet over high heat. Season the filets with the peppercorn mixture. Sear the filets for 3 to 4 minutes on each side for rare to medium-rare. Add the thyme, garlic, and butter; once sizzling, baste the filets, then remove them from the pan. Let rest for 1 to 2 minutes before serving.

To serve, divide the olive oil mash among 4 plates. Place a filet on top of the potatoes. Serve with a large spoonful of the roasted chili and olive ragout.

For the Sun-Dried Tomato Tapenade

1 cup (250 mL) oil-packed sun-dried tomatoes
½ cup (125 mL) pitted olives
¼ cup (60 mL) basil leaves
2 tbsp (30 mL) capers
Zest and juice of 1 lemon
2 cloves garlic, chopped
Salt and pepper

For the Salmon and Ratatouille Provençale

¼ cup (60 mL) olive oil
1 red onion, chopped
2 cloves garlic, minced
1 tsp (5 mL) thyme leaves
1 small eggplant, cut into 1-inch (2.5 cm) cubes
1 red bell pepper, seeded and cut into 1-inch (2.5 cm) pieces
1 yellow bell pepper, seeded and cut into 1-inch (2.5 cm) pieces
2 medium zucchini, cut into 1-inch (2.5 cm) cubes
1 can (14 oz/398 mL) chopped tomatoes
1 tbsp (15 mL) chopped basil
1 tbsp (15 mL) chopped parsley
4 skinless salmon fillets (each 6 oz/175 g)
Salt and pepper

SALMON & RATATOUILLE PROVENÇALE

This tapenade is great on moist and tender salmon, but it is also fantastic on grilled bread or even in a pasta salad. The salty olives and the sweet sun-dried tomatoes work so well together. It is one of the most versatile recipes I know.

Serves 4

To make the tapenade, put all the tapenade ingredients in a food processor. Blend until a moist paste forms. Add extra-virgin olive oil if too dry. Season with salt and pepper. Set aside.

To make the salmon and ratatouille, preheat your oven to 375°F (190°C). Heat the oil in a large heatproof casserole dish over medium heat. Add the onions, garlic, and thyme; cook, stirring often, for 5 minutes or until the onions caramelize. Add the eggplant and red and yellow peppers; continue to cook for 5 minutes. Add the zucchini, tomatoes, basil, and parsley; stir together well. Season the salmon with salt and pepper. Place the salmon on top of the ratatouille. Cover and bake until the fish is firm to the touch and opaque, 15 to 20 minutes. Remove from oven and divide the ratatouille among 4 plates.

Serve the salmon on the ratatouille, topped with a dollop of tapenade.

ORANGES

Don't underestimate the orange! That was the theme that came out of my visit to an orange grove in Crescent City, Florida. There's more to sunny oranges than you think. They're incredibly versatile. I remember talking to two of my favourite people on this trip, Mr. Jones and Jabo, both long-time orange harvesters, about whether they used oranges in their food. A glass of orange juice at breakfast was about all they ever had. So I was on a mission.

What I love most about oranges is their sweet smell. It migrates into any food you cook using this fruit. The oils in the rind can be tart, the juice and flesh is sweet, and the sugars caramelize to a sensational burnt-orange flavour when roasted.

Where there are oranges, there are bees, and where there are bees, there's honey. Orange blossom honey is truly something unique: fruity and yummy—so sweet that it tingles the tip of your tongue when you taste it. A perfect accompaniment for Florida's perfect fruit.

VEAL CHOPS WITH CITRUS SALAD

I made this recipe in an orange grove in Crescent City, Florida, with some orange pickers I worked with, Mr. Jones and Jabo. Their reaction was something I'll never forget. They absolutely loved it! Essentially a breaded veal chop, this is fun fine dining. Serve with a roasted tangerine and a peppery salad of watercress, orange, and fennel.

Serves 4

For the Veal Chops
1 cup (250 mL) orange juice
2 tbsp (30 mL) Dijon mustard
2 shallots, thinly sliced
4 bone-in veal chops (each 10 oz/300 g), pounded to ¼-inch (5 mm) thickness
1 cup (250 mL) all-purpose flour
4 large eggs
2 cups (500 mL) panko bread crumbs
Salt and pepper
½ cup (125 mL) olive oil
1 tbsp (15 mL) sugar
2 tangerines, cut in half crosswise

For the Watercress and Fennel Salad
1 bunch watercress
1 head frisée, torn
1 fennel bulb, thinly shaved
3 oranges, peeled and cut into segments
Citrus Vinaigrette (page 257)
Salt and pepper

To start the veal chops, in a shallow dish large enough to hold the chops in one layer, stir together the orange juice, mustard, and shallots. Add the veal chops, turning to coat in the marinade. Cover and refrigerate for 20 minutes. Put the flour in a shallow bowl. In a second shallow bowl, beat the eggs. In a third bowl, combine the bread crumbs with the salt and pepper. Remove a veal chop from the marinade, allowing excess liquid to drip off. Dredge the veal chop in the flour, shaking off excess. Dip into the egg mixture, and then cover with bread crumbs. Repeat with remaining chops.

Heat the oil in a large skillet over medium heat. When the oil is hot, cook the chops until golden brown, about 3 minutes on each side. Transfer to paper towels to absorb any excess oil.

Heat a small skillet over medium-high heat. Sprinkle the sugar on the cut sides of the tangerines. Place tangerines cut side down in the pan and cook, pressing down, until caramelized. Remove with tongs and set aside.

To make the salad, in a large bowl, combine the watercress, frisée, fennel, and orange segments. Toss with the citrus vinaigrette. Season with salt and pepper.

To serve, place a veal chop on each plate and top with the salad. Serve with the brûléed tangerine halves.

GLAZED QUAIL WITH PECAN & ORANGE SALAD

Some combinations of flavours were just meant to be delicious. In this dish, the spiced, sweet, nutty pecans come alive with the pomegranate-molasses-marinated quail.

Serves 4

For the Glazed Quail

4 semi-boneless quail

¼ cup (60 mL) pomegranate molasses

¼ cup (60 mL) honey

Juice of 1 orange

1 tsp (5 mL) thyme leaves

Salt and pepper

For the Spiced Cheyenne Pecans
(makes 2 cups/500 mL)

2 tsp (10 mL) salt

2 tsp (10 mL) five-spice powder

2 tsp (10 mL) cinnamon

2 tsp (10 mL) ground ginger

2 tsp (10 mL) ground cumin

1 tsp (5 mL) chili powder

1 large egg white

2 cups (500 mL) Cheyenne pecan halves

For the Spiced Pecan and Orange Salad

2 cups (500 mL) chopped frisée

4 endives, chopped

1 radicchio, chopped

2 oranges, peeled and cut into segments

¼ cup (60 mL) spiced Cheyenne pecans

Pecan Pomegranate Vinaigrette
   (page 257)

Salt and pepper

Rinse the quail and pat them dry. To butterfly the quail, cut along both sides of the backbone with kitchen shears and discard backbone. Open them up and thread a wooden skewer from the bottom of the leg to the top of the breast on each side to hold their shape flat. In a small baking dish, whisk together the pomegranate molasses, honey, orange juice, and thyme. Add the quail, turning to coat, and marinate, covered and refrigerated, for about 2 hours.

Meanwhile, make the spiced pecans. Preheat your oven to 225°F (110°C). Line a large baking sheet with parchment paper. In a small bowl, stir together the salt and all the spices. In a large bowl, whisk the egg white until foamy. Whisk in the spice mixture. Add the pecans and toss to coat completely. Spread the pecans in a single layer on the baking sheet. Bake, stirring every 20 minutes, until the nuts are toasted and the coating is dry, about 1 hour. Set aside ¼ cup for the salad. Remaining pecans will keep in an airtight container for up to 1 week.

Preheat your grill to medium-high. Remove the quail from the marinade and set aside. Pour the marinade into a small pot. Cook over medium heat until the liquid is reduced to a glaze, about 15 minutes.

Meanwhile, make the salad. In a large bowl, combine the frisée, endives, radicchio, orange segments, spiced pecans, and pecan pomegranate vinaigrette. Season with salt and pepper and toss well.

Season the quail with salt and pepper. Grill the quail for about 4 minutes per side, basting frequently with the glaze.

Remove the skewers from the quail. Serve with the salad.

Here's an idea: Chicken breast is another option instead of using quail.

PECANS

Everybody knows a cook with a special, closely guarded, top-secret recipe. Maybe you have one or two of your own. In Texas, or anywhere in the South, that recipe is usually for some seriously incredible pecan pie. I managed to score a secret recipe for pecan pie, and let me tell you, it's one of the finest I've ever had.

Beyond pies, wonderful though they are, pecans can stand tall among many different foods because of their full, rich flavour. Sweet dishes are obviously a perfect home for these nuts, but savoury can be fabulous too—on a salad, toasted with meat or fish, or paired with winter squash or sweet potatoes. Perfection.

There are several types of pecans, so keep an eye open for different varieties to try out. Natives are small and less sweet with a big crunch, Stuarts are a little lower in oils, and Choctaws are those great big super-buttery nuts that just scream "eat me!"

Play around with pecans and maybe you can develop a secret recipe of your own. Even if it doesn't stay secret, you can still call it your secret recipe, which will just add to the allure.

PECAN-BUTTER-BASTED BEEF TENDERLOIN

Sweet and nutty pecan butter is absolutely fantastic on beef, fish, or chicken. Add a tablespoon or two of the pecan butter at the last moment of cooking and elevate your dish to a whole new level.

Serves 4

For the Beef Tenderloin

½ cup (125 mL) unsalted butter, softened
¼ cup (60 mL) toasted pecans, finely chopped
2 tbsp (30 mL) olive oil
4 beef tenderloin filets (each 6 oz/175 g)
Salt and pepper
4 shallots, thinly sliced
2 cups (500 mL) chanterelle mushrooms, thinly sliced
¼ cup (60 mL) red wine
1 cup (250 mL) roasted chicken stock (page 245)
1 sprig thyme

For the Sweet Potato Pecan Cakes

1 lb (500 g) sweet potatoes
½ cup (125 mL) all-purpose flour
¼ cup (60 mL) pecans, toasted and finely chopped
2 tbsp (30 mL) finely chopped parsley
1 bunch green onions, thinly sliced
Salt and pepper
2 tbsp (30 mL) olive oil

For the Creamed Spinach and Pecans

2 tbsp (30 mL) unsalted butter
2 shallots, finely chopped
1 medium clove garlic, minced
¼ cup (60 mL) pecans, finely chopped
1 cup (250 mL) heavy cream
½ cup (125 mL) grated Parmesan cheese
⅛ tsp (0.5 mL) nutmeg
1 lb (500 g) baby spinach, washed, dried, and stems removed
Salt and pepper

In a small bowl, mash together the butter and pecans until well combined. Heat the olive oil in a medium-sized, heavy skillet over medium-high heat. Season the filets with salt and pepper. Cook the filets for 4 minutes on the first side. Turn over and cook for 2 minutes, then add half of the pecan butter. Continue cooking and basting for another 2 minutes. Remove the filets from the pan and let rest.

In the same pan, over medium-high heat, cook the shallots and mushrooms, stirring often, until the mushrooms are tender, about 4 minutes. Remove from the pan and set aside. Deglaze the pan with the wine and cook until reduced by half, about 2 minutes. Add the stock and thyme; bring to a boil. Reduce heat to medium and simmer, stirring occasionally, for 8 minutes to blend the flavours. Strain the sauce through a fine-mesh strainer into a small saucepan; discard the solids. Add the reserved mushrooms and remaining pecan butter to the sauce and whisk together. Season well with salt and pepper.

Put the sweet potatoes in a large pot of cold, salted water and bring to a boil. Cook until the potatoes are tender, about 30 minutes. Drain and let cool. Peel the potatoes, then coarsely grate them into a large bowl. Add the flour, pecans, parsley, green onions, and salt and pepper to taste; mix together well. Heat the oil in a large nonstick skillet over medium-high heat. Form the potatoes into four cakes. Working in batches, fry the potato cakes until golden brown, 2 to 3 minutes per side.

For the cream sauce, in a medium saucepan, melt the butter over medium heat. Gently sauté the shallots until translucent. Stir in the garlic and pecans and cook for another minute. Pour in the cream and bring to a simmer. Stir in the Parmesan and nutmeg. Gently simmer, stirring often, until the sauce thickens, about 5 minutes.

After the sauce has thickened, add the spinach to the cream and turn up the heat to medium-high. Cook the spinach in the reduced cream until just wilted, about 2 minutes. Season with salt and pepper.

To serve, divide the creamed spinach and sweet potato cakes onto four plates. Place the beef filets on top of the creamed spinach and top with sauce.

ON THE FARM

CRISPY CHICKEN EGG SALAD

Which came first, the chicken or the egg? In this salad they shine together and make that age-old question seem unimportant. Crispy golden fried nuggets of tender, buttermilk-marinated thigh meat are paired with a watercress and radish salad and a soft-boiled hen's egg. Topping it all off is a fennel chow-chow inspired by my time in North Carolina, where they put it on everything! The recipe for fennel chow-chow will make more than you need for the salad, but it is great to have on hand as a condiment for lunch and dinner.

Serves 4

For the Crispy Chicken
2 boneless skinless chicken thighs, cubed
1 cup (250 mL) buttermilk
2 cups (500 mL) vegetable oil
2 cups (500 mL) all-purpose flour
1 tbsp (15 mL) salt
1 tbsp (15 mL) pepper
2 cups (500 mL) vegetable oil

For the Salad
4 large eggs
2 cups (500 mL) watercress
½ cup (125 mL) thinly sliced radishes
¼ cup Sherry Shallot Vinaigrette
   (page 256)
Salt and pepper
¼ cup (60 mL) Fennel Chow-Chow
Gribiche Sauce (page 252)

For the Fennel Chow-Chow
(makes 4 cups/1 L)
1 cup (250 mL) rice wine vinegar
½ cup (125 mL) water
¼ cup (60 mL) sugar
1 tsp (5 mL) salt
¼ tsp (1 mL) pickling spice
¼ tsp (1 mL) mustard seeds
2 bay leaves
1 large fennel bulb, thinly sliced
1 red onion, thinly sliced
1 English cucumber, sliced

Marinate the chicken in the buttermilk for 1 hour, covered in the refrigerator.

While the chicken is marinating, make the fennel chow-chow. In a large saucepan, combine the vinegar, water, sugar, salt, pickling spice, mustard seeds, and bay leaves. Bring to a boil, stirring until the sugar is dissolved. Cover and simmer for 30 minutes. In a bowl, combine the fennel, onion, and cucumber. Strain the hot liquid over the vegetables. Let cool at room temperature, then cover and chill.

Next, boil the eggs for the salad. Bring a pot of salted water to a boil. Place the eggs in the water and cook for 6 minutes. Remove with a slotted spoon and chill in a bowl of ice water. Peel the eggs and cut in half lengthwise; set aside.

To cook the chicken, in a large pot, heat the oil over medium-high heat to 350°F (180°C). In a bowl, combine the flour, salt, and pepper. Remove the chicken from the buttermilk and roll it in the flour. Carefully add the chicken to the hot oil and cook until golden brown, 3 to 4 minutes. Drain on paper towels.

To finish the salad, toss the watercress and radishes with the vinaigrette. Season with salt and pepper.

To serve, divide the salad among 4 salad plates. Top with the fennel chow-chow and the chicken. Garnish with the soft-boiled eggs and gribiche sauce.

STICKY HONEY GARLIC CHICKEN WINGS

One of my Sri Lankan cooks introduced me to Sriracha sauce years ago. He put it on everything and he soon had me hooked. This bright red chili and garlic paste from Thailand is seriously addictive. Feel free to up the amount in this recipe, my favourite one for sticky, delicious wings. How much heat can you handle?

Serves 4

½ cup (125 mL) soy sauce
¼ cup (60 mL) honey
2 tbsp (30 mL) dark brown sugar
2 tbsp (30 mL) grated orange zest
2 tbsp (30 mL) minced garlic
1 tbsp (15 mL) minced ginger

1 tbsp (15 mL) Sriracha chili sauce
1 tbsp (15 mL) black pepper
2 lb (1 kg) chicken wings
1 bunch green onions, thinly sliced, for garnish

In a large bowl, combine the soy sauce, honey, brown sugar, orange zest, garlic, ginger, Sriracha sauce, and black pepper. Add the wings and toss to coat well. Cover and refrigerate for at least 2 hours or overnight.

Preheat your oven to 425°F (220°C). Arrange the wings on a rack in a shallow roasting pan. Bake the wings for about 40 minutes, turning them occasionally and brushing them with the remaining marinade when you turn them. Cook until the skin is dark brown and crispy. Arrange on a platter, sprinkle with the green onions, and serve.

¼ cup (60 mL) unsalted butter
¾ cup (175 mL) finely chopped shallots
1 clove garlic, minced
1 lb (500 g) chicken livers, trimmed
Salt and pepper

2 tsp (10 mL) finely chopped thyme
¼ cup (60 mL) brandy
¼ tsp (1 mL) nutmeg
Pinch allspice

Melt the butter in a large sauté pan over medium heat. Add the shallots and garlic and cook until softened, about 5 minutes. Season the livers with salt and pepper. Add to the pan and cook, stirring, until almost cooked through but still slightly pink inside, about 10 minutes. Add the thyme and brandy; simmer until most of the brandy has evaporated. Transfer to a food processor. Add the nutmeg and allspice. Process until very smooth, about 1 minute. Season well with salt and pepper.

Transfer the pâté to an airtight container or ramekins. Press plastic wrap directly on the surface and refrigerate until firm.

Serve with country baguette.

CHICKEN LIVER PÂTÉ

The best thing about this recipe is that it sounds fancy and never fails to wow, yet at the same time it is one of the simplest to have in your repertoire. Also, there's brandy in it. Enough said.

Serves 6 to 8

WILD BOAR BACON SALAD

When I discovered wild boar bacon, I became slightly obsessed with it, and I guarantee that as soon as you taste it, you will too. Seek it out at farmer's markets, buy as much as you can, and freeze it so that you always have some on hand. This recipe doesn't just have bacon in the salad—it's in the vinaigrette too. I told you I was obsessed.

Serves 4

For the Balsamic Reduction
¾ cup (175 mL) balsamic vinegar

For the Wild Boar Bacon Salad
½ cup (125 mL) diced wild boar bacon
3 shallots, quartered
1 cup (250 mL) cherry tomatoes, cut in halves or quarters
3 tbsp (50 mL) sherry vinegar
¼ cup (60 mL) olive oil
2 tbsp (30 mL) chopped parsley
2 tbsp (30 mL) chopped chives
Salt and pepper
3 cups (750 mL) torn frisée
4 slices wild boar bacon (about ½-inch/1 cm thick)

First make the balsamic reduction. Place the balsamic vinegar in a small saucepan and boil until reduced to 3 tbsp (50 mL), 6 to 7 minutes.

In a heavy saucepan, cook the diced bacon over medium heat, stirring occasionally, until golden and crispy, about 5 minutes. Reduce heat to low, then add the shallots; cook for another 2 minutes, or until shallots are tender. Add the cherry tomatoes and sherry vinegar and reduce liquid by half. Remove from heat and stir in the olive oil. Season the vinaigrette with salt and pepper and keep warm.

In a heavy skillet over medium-low heat, cook the 4 thick wild boar bacon slices until golden brown, about 3 minutes per side.

Toss the frisée with the parsley and chives, then toss with the warm vinaigrette.

To serve, place a slice of wild boar bacon on each plate. Divide the salad evenly among the plates. Drizzle with balsamic reduction.

Here's an idea: If you can't get your hands on wild boar bacon, look for maple smoked bacon.

For the Turkey Wing Vinaigrette
(makes 1 cup/500 mL)

1 tbsp (30 mL) olive oil

2 turkey wings (or 6 chicken wings),
    chopped into 1-inch (2.5 cm) pieces

2 cloves garlic, chopped

2 shallots, thinly sliced

1 sprig thyme

1 bay leaf

¼ cup (60 mL) sherry vinegar

1 cup (250 mL) chicken stock (page 245)

3 tbsp (50 mL) hazelnut oil

2 tbsp (30 mL) finely chopped parsley

Salt and pepper

For the Turkey Club Salad

½ lb (250 g) turkey breast, sliced
    crosswise into 4 slices

1 egg

½ cup (125 mL) dried bread crumbs

2 tbsp (30 mL) chopped parsley

1 tbsp (15 mL) all-purpose flour

1 tsp (5 mL) salt

¼ cup (60 mL) vegetable oil

8 slices turkey bacon

2 beefsteak tomatoes, sliced

Salt and pepper

Leaves from 1 head butter lettuce

1 avocado, peeled and thinly sliced

½ cup (125 mL) cherry tomatoes,
    sliced, for garnish

TURKEY CLUB SALAD

Here's a deconstructed version of the diner classic that goes places no ordinary clubhouse sandwich has ever been. Golden fried turkey, ripe beefsteak tomatoes, turkey bacon, avocado, and butter lettuce get drizzled in a rich, lip-smacking turkey wing vinaigrette. Your life will never be the same.

Serves 4

To make the turkey wing vinaigrette, in a large skillet over medium heat combine the olive oil and turkey wings. Cook the wings, stirring occasionally, until golden brown, about 12 minutes. Add the garlic, shallots, thyme, and bay leaf; cook, stirring occasionally, until the shallots are translucent. Deglaze with 3 tbsp (50 mL) of the sherry vinegar and cook down until it has almost evaporated. Add the chicken stock; simmer until reduced to ¾ cup (175 mL). Strain through a fine-mesh sieve into a small bowl. Whisk in the hazelnut oil and remaining sherry vinegar. Stir in the parsley and season with salt and pepper. Set aside, keeping warm.

To begin the salad, pound the turkey slices between 2 sheets of plastic wrap until thin. In a shallow bowl, lightly beat the egg with 1 tbsp (15 mL) water. In a second shallow bowl, combine the bread crumbs, parsley, flour, and salt. Dip the turkey cutlets in the egg, then coat with the bread crumb mixture.

In a large skillet over medium-high heat, heat the vegetable oil. Cook the turkey cutlets one at a time until golden brown and cooked through, 3 to 4 minutes on each side. Meanwhile, in another skillet over medium heat, cook the turkey bacon until crisp.

Season the tomato slices with salt and pepper. Place tomato slices onto the 4 serving plates and top with turkey bacon. Place the lettuce on top of the bacon and top with the turkey cutlets and cherry tomatoes. Garnish with the avocado slices and drizzle the salad with the warm vinaigrette.

CHICKEN

I love chicken and I love eggs, and I'll tell you I don't know which I love first, but what I do know is this: when it comes to chickens and eggs, all are not created equal.

I went to Siler City, North Carolina, to an organic, heritage chicken farm to experience first-hand the fabulous Poulet Rouge breed. This naked-necked bird may not be the most attractive in the coop, but it sure is the prom queen when it comes to taste. At Joyce Farms, the chickens are lovingly, carefully raised and are truly free range. As a result, the meat is juicier, thicker, and more flavourful than your average supermarket bird.

While I was on the farm, my host, Darrell Harris, gave me the opportunity to try some of the eggs he had gathered that morning. We made eggs over easy scramble—and wow, the taste was out of this world. The yolks are so bright, so rich and delicious, simplicity at its best. You can taste, and even see, good quality, which is no surprise.

When an animal is naturally and compassionately raised, you'll definitely taste that in your cooking. I always like to get the best free-range bird possible and then roast or fry it to perfection. Respecting your food and being aware of where your products come from has never been easier and can rightly be a source of pride.

LEMON THYME ROASTED CHICKEN & POLENTA

Inspired by the Zuni Café, this is the best roast chicken I know how to make. When you pay extra for a chicken that's been fed right and raised in the sunshine, you want to treat it with respect. Serve it up with an inviting rustic pumpernickel panzanella and a silky mascarpone polenta, and you'll never go back to chicken and mashed potatoes.

Serves 4 to 6

For the Lemon Thyme Roasted Chicken

2 lemons
Leaves from 3 sprigs thyme, chopped
2 tbsp (30 mL) olive oil, plus more
    for drizzling
2 cloves garlic, finely chopped
Salt and pepper
1 chicken (7 lb/3.15 kg)
2 onions, sliced
2 heads garlic, cut in half crosswise
¼ cup (60 mL) dry white wine
1 cup (250 mL) chicken stock (page 245)
2 tbsp (30 mL) unsalted butter
2 tbsp (30 mL) chopped parsley

For the Creamy Polenta

4 to 5 cups (1 to 1.25 L) chicken stock
3 tbsp (50 mL) unsalted butter
1½ cups (375 mL) cornmeal
½ cup (125 mL) mascarpone cheese
¼ cup (60 mL) grated Parmesan cheese
3 tbsp (50 mL) chopped parsley
Salt and pepper

For the Mustard Greens Panzanella Salad

4 cups (1 L) pumpernickel bread torn into
    1-inch (2.5 cm) pieces
3 tbsp (50 mL) extra-virgin olive oil
2 tbsp (30 mL) grated Parmesan cheese
Salt and pepper
2 sweet potatoes, peeled and cut into
    ½-inch (1 cm) cubes
1 radicchio, leaves torn
4 cups (1 L) mustard greens
¼ cup (60 mL) basil leaves
½ cup Sherry Shallot Vinaigrette
    (page 256)
Fleur de sel

To roast the chicken, preheat your oven to 375°F (190°C). Zest the lemons; set aside the zest. Squeeze the juice from the lemons (reserve for another use) and set aside the lemon halves. In a large bowl, combine the lemon zest, thyme, olive oil, chopped garlic, and salt and pepper. Add the chicken and turn to coat well on all sides. Season the cavity well with salt and pepper and stuff with the reserved lemon halves.

Spread the sliced onions in a roasting pan. Place the chicken on the onions. Add the heads of garlic, cut sides up, and drizzle them with some olive oil. Roast the chicken at 375°F for ½ hour then turn down the oven to 350°F, basting occasionally, and cook for about 1 hour, or until the skin is golden brown and crisp and the juices run clear when the chicken is pierced with a knife at the joint of the leg. Transfer the chicken and roasted garlic to a platter and cover loosely with foil to keep warm.

Continued

Start making the polenta about an hour after the chicken has been roasting. Bring 4 cups (1 L) of the chicken stock and the butter to a boil in a large saucepan. Reduce heat to medium. Slowly whisk in the cornmeal. Cook, whisking occasionally, for about 20 minutes, until the polenta is creamy and adding more stock ¼ cup (60 mL) at a time as necessary to keep the polenta soft. Remove from heat. Stir in the mascarpone, Parmesan, and parsley. Season with salt and pepper. Keep warm.

After the chicken is removed from the roasting pan, put the pan on the stovetop over medium-high heat. Add the wine and bring to a boil, scraping up any browned bits. Add the chicken stock and boil until reduced by half. Strain the pan sauce into a small pot and whisk in the butter and parsley. Season with salt and pepper. Keep warm.

To make the salad, toss the bread with 2 tbsp (30 mL) of the olive oil, the Parmesan, and salt and pepper. Spread the bread on a baking sheet and bake for 5 minutes, until slightly crisp. Transfer to a large bowl. Toss the sweet potatoes with the remaining oil; season with salt and pepper. Spread on the baking sheet and roast until soft, about 15 minutes. While the sweet potatoes are roasting, carve the chicken. Add the sweet potatoes to the bread cubes. Add the radicchio, mustard greens, and basil. Toss with the vinaigrette.

To serve, carve the chicken. Spoon a bed of warm polenta onto each plate and top with some chicken. Spoon some pan sauce over and around the polenta and chicken. Season the chicken with fleur de sel and serve the panzanella alongside.

1 tbsp (15 mL) coriander seeds
1 tbsp (15 mL) fennel seeds
2 tsp (10 mL) pink peppercorns
½ tsp (2 mL) cumin seeds
1 whole clove
2 tbsp (30 mL) salt
1 tsp (5 mL) ground allspice
2 lb (1 kg) pork belly
4 sprigs thyme, roughly chopped

2 sprigs rosemary, roughly chopped
4 Gala apples, cored and cut into 1-inch
   (2.5 cm) slices
2 onions, cut into 1-inch (2.5 cm) slices
1 cup (250 mL) chicken stock (page 245)
1 cup (250 mL) apple cider
½ cup (125 mL) maple syrup
Salt and pepper

APPLE CIDER PORK BELLY

Not many people make pork belly at home, and I want to change that. Step away from the chops and roasts you're so used to and take a chance on a cut that has long been ignored. Simply rubbed with a spiced salt and then braised over sliced Gala apples with apple cider and maple syrup, these are the most heavenly bites you will ever put in your mouth.

Serves 4 to 6

Preheat your oven to 425°F (220°C). In a sauté pan over medium heat, toast the coriander seeds, fennel seeds, peppercorns, cumin seeds, and clove for a few minutes, until fragrant. Grind the spices together and place in a small bowl. Stir in the salt and allspice.

Score the skin of the pork belly with a sharp knife. Rub the belly all over with spice blend, thyme, and rosemary, getting the seasonings into the cracks.

Layer the apples and onions in a roasting pan, then place the pork belly skin side up on top. Pour the chicken stock, apple cider, and maple syrup into the pan. Cover tightly with foil and roast for 1 hour. Turn the oven down to 350°F (180°C), remove the foil, and cook for another hour, or until the juices run clear when the meat is pierced with a knife.

Remove the pork belly from the pan and remove the crackling from the pork before carving. Add the apples, onions, and cooking liquid into a blender and purée until smooth. Pass through a strainer into a serving bowl. Carve the pork belly and serve with apple sauce.

You could also serve with mashed potatoes and butter-roasted carrots.

PORK

I love pork. I love bacon, and prosciutto, and ribs, and chops.... Did I mention I love pork? It's hard to go wrong with this tasty meat, so I set out to find the very best of all.

My search for the perfect pig landed me in Dixie, Georgia, with farmers Andrew and Jennifer Thompson. It just doesn't get any more southern than Dixie, my friends and pig farming is truly something else. Sure, the piglets are cute, but then there's the boars and the sows. Not so cute, and mean too. But to-beat-the-band delicious.

If there's any one thing to remember when you're cooking pork, especially good quality pork and a good cut, it's to *leave it alone.* You don't need to mess with it!

No brining, no marinating, no messing about. Make a simple plan and let the pork shine on its own.

They say barbecue sauce runs in a Southerner's blood. And so we can't talk about pork and the South and not mention barbecue. Right? I mean, come on! Down in Dixie, I had the honour of meeting Jimmy Vicker, a South Georgia barbecue *legend*. When I asked Jimmy how he did what he did, because it was just so perfect, I learned that, like any of us with a deep passion, Jimmy was born with his love of barbecue. As he said, "This is it. This is what I do."

Amen, brother Jimmy! Let's bring our passion to pork.

For the Collard Greens

1¼ lb (625 g) collard greens
2 tbsp (30 mL) olive oil
2 thick slices smoked bacon, diced
1 small onion, finely chopped
2 tbsp (30 mL) finely chopped garlic
⅛ tsp (0.5 mL) chili flakes
1 tbsp (15 mL) cider vinegar
2 tbsp (30 mL) maple syrup
2 cups (500 mL) chicken stock
    (page 245)
Salt and pepper

For the Cider-Glazed Pork Chops

2 tbsp (30 mL) olive oil
4 boneless centre-cut pork chops
    (each 1½ inches/4 cm thick)
Salt and pepper
2 tbsp (30 mL) unsalted butter
2 cloves garlic, crushed
2 sprigs thyme

For the Apple Thyme Chutney

1 tbsp (15 mL) unsalted butter
1 large onion, finely chopped
4 green apples, peeled, cored,
    and cut into ½-inch (1 cm) cubes
¼ cup (60 mL) cider vinegar
2 tbsp (30 mL) dark brown sugar
1 tbsp (15 mL) grainy mustard
1 tsp (5 mL) chopped thyme
Salt and pepper

CIDER-GLAZED PORK CHOPS

Apple cider, thyme, brown sugar, and mustard come together to glaze these juicy chops. Serve them up with collard greens cooked with smoky bacon and maple syrup and you're taking comfort food to a whole new level.

Serves 4

To prepare the collard greens, remove and discard the stems and centre ribs. Cut the leaves into ½-inch (1 cm) strips. Heat the olive oil in a large pot over medium heat. Add the bacon, onions, garlic, and chili flakes; cook, stirring occasionally, until the onions are softened. Add the cider vinegar, maple syrup, and chicken stock; bring to a boil. Add the collard greens and season with salt and pepper. Stir together well. Reduce heat to a simmer, cover, and cook for 20 minutes or until greens are wilted.

About halfway through simmering the collard greens, cook the chops. Preheat your oven to 375°F (190°C). Heat the olive oil in an ovenproof skillet over medium-high heat. Season the pork chops with salt and pepper. Sear the chops until golden brown, about 2 minutes per side. Add the butter, garlic, and thyme to the pan. Baste the chops with the sizzling butter, then transfer to the oven and roast for 8 to 10 minutes. Remove from oven and let rest for 5 minutes before serving.

While the chops are roasting, make the chutney. In a medium saucepan, melt the butter over medium heat. Add the onions and cook, stirring often, until caramelized, about 8 minutes. Add the apples, vinegar, brown sugar, mustard, and thyme. Stir well to combine. Cook for about 3 minutes, until the apples have softened. Season with salt and pepper.

To serve, divide the collard greens among 4 plates. Top with a pork chop. Spoon the chutney over the chops.

TURKEY

I went to the heartland of America to find out about
heritage-breed turkeys and how they're raised. I bet you
think raising a free-range bird would be easy, right? Just
let the bird go and do its thing, then catch it when it's
ready for market. Yeah, well, not so much. I worked my
pants off on that job.

What I'll tell you is that free-range turkeys are so far
superior to commercially raised birds that the difference
is almost night and day. First, free-range birds can fly,
run around, and mate naturally, so they have much greater
muscle mass. This means denser meat, which is much
richer in colour and flavour. It doesn't matter how you like
to cook your turkey, you're going to have a better dish
when you start with a better bird. End of story.

For the dinner I prepared on that first adventure,
I really wanted to be sure I used the whole bird in my meal,
to get the most out of what I was discovering. You can
smoke, confit, roast, fry, boil, and broil all with the same
bird—each method has its own rewards, and all will mesh
together to create one memorably sumptuous feast.

TURKEY WITH MAPLE SWEET POTATOES

Here I've basically taken the method behind duck confit and put it into practice on some turkey legs. It's not unusual to spend an outrageous amount of time preparing a traditional turkey for the holidays, so why not take a more leisurely route and confit the bird for a new and luxurious spin on a classic holiday dinner.

Serves 4

For the Turkey Leg Confit

4 sprigs thyme, chopped
2 sprigs sage, chopped
2 bay leaves
3 cloves garlic, crushed
½ cup (125 mL) kosher salt
2 tsp (10 mL) cracked black peppercorns
4 heritage turkey legs, thighs and drumsticks separated
8 cups (2 L) duck fat, melted
1 cup (250 mL) Quick Turkey Gravy (page 248)

For the Maple Whipped Sweet Potatoes

2 lb (1 kg) sweet potatoes
¼ cup (60 mL) unsalted butter
½ cup (125 mL) heavy cream, warmed
2 tbsp (30 mL) maple syrup
Salt and pepper

To make the turkey confit, combine the thyme, sage, bay leaves, garlic, salt, and peppercorns. Place the turkey in a large pan. Rub the turkey all over with the herb mixture. Cover and refrigerate for 6 to 8 hours.

Preheat your oven to 325°F (160°C). Rinse the turkey and pat dry; transfer to a roasting pan just large enough to hold them. Melt the duck fat in a large pot over medium-high heat. Pour the duck fat over the turkey. The duck fat should just cover the meat. Cover with foil. Bake until the meat is very tender and falls easily from the bone, about 3 hours. Remove from the pan and let cool slightly, then remove and discard the skin and bones. Set aside the meat and keep warm.

Bake the sweet potatoes until very tender, about 1½ hours, while the turkey is cooking. Let cool slightly, then halve the potatoes lengthwise and scoop the warm flesh into a large pot. Mash the potatoes, then stir in the butter, cream, and maple syrup. Season with salt and pepper and keep warm.

To serve, place the sweet potatoes onto dinner plates and top with turkey and gravy. Perfect with peas and carrots on the side for a dinner classic.

For the Turkey Casserole

1 boneless skinless turkey breast
(about 1½ lb/750 g)
4 cups (1 L) chicken stock (page 245)
¼ cup (60 mL) unsalted butter
1 onion, finely diced
3 carrots, cut into ½-inch (1 cm) slices
1 stalk celery, cut into ½-inch (1 cm)
slices
1 cup (250 mL) quartered button
mushrooms
⅓ cup (75 mL) all-purpose flour
1 tbsp (15 mL) finely chopped parsley
1 tbsp (15 mL) finely chopped dill
Salt and pepper

For the Cheddar Biscuits

2 cups (500 mL) all-purpose flour
1 tbsp (15 mL) baking powder
1 tsp (5 mL) sugar
1 tsp (5 mL) salt
½ cup (125 mL) cold unsalted butter,
cut into small pieces
2 tbsp (30 mL) grated aged Cheddar
2 tbsp (30 mL) finely chopped chives
¾ cup (175 mL) milk, plus more
for brushing

TURKEY CASSEROLE WITH BISCUITS

My mom always made turkey casseroles, like turkey à la king, which was the inspiration for this recipe. Deeply flavourful poached heritage turkey breast in a rich stock with mushrooms and celery and topped with Cheddar and chive biscuits makes a beautiful dish to bring to the table.

Serves 4

To make the casserole, put the turkey breast in a medium saucepan. Add enough chicken stock to just cover it and bring to a boil. Reduce heat to very low and poach the turkey until it is just firm to the touch, about 30 minutes. Remove the turkey from the stock (reserve the stock) and when cool enough to handle, cut into large bite-size pieces.

Preheat your oven to 450°F (230°C). In a large saucepan, melt the butter over medium-high heat. Add the onions, carrots, and celery; cook, stirring often, until the vegetables are light brown, about 4 minutes. Add the mushrooms and cook for 2 minutes. Add the flour and cook, stirring, for another minute. Pour in the reserved stock and whisk until it comes to a boil. Reduce heat slightly and simmer until thick, about 3 minutes. Remove from heat. Stir in the turkey, parsley, and dill; season with salt and pepper. Pour into a large rectangular baking dish.

To make the biscuits, in a large bowl, combine the flour, baking powder, sugar, and salt. Using your fingertips, rub the butter into the flour until it forms pea-size pieces. Add the cheese and chives. Stir in the milk to make a soft dough.

On a lightly floured surface, roll out the dough into a rectangle ½ inch (1 cm) thick. Cut dough into 2-inch (5 cm) square biscuits. Arrange the biscuits over the turkey filling. Brush the biscuits lightly with milk. Put the baking dish on a baking sheet and bake until golden brown on top, about 20 minutes.

Serve the casserole family style with a big salad.

WILD BOAR

As soon as I decided to check out boar farming, I became obsessed with the idea of making wild boar bacon. I'd never had it before and I just had a feeling it was going to be terrific.

Wild boar is the original pork, dating back thousands of years. Boar takes three years to get to market, whereas commercial pork takes only about six months. And I'll tell you something: those extra two and a half years of eating black walnuts and grains and running around the farm create a meatier, more flavourful dish with incredible marbling.

In Stratford, Ontario, I attended a dinner roast of a whole wild boar. The instant the boar was off the spit, I dove straight into the belly, and to my excitement, found perfect bacon potential there. I found a great butcher to prepare the most fantastic slab of boar bacon for me. From the first taste, I knew this was everything I'd hoped it would be and more. I gathered my farmer friends and the butcher, and fed a full circle of guests.

Boar is delicious and has just the right edge of exotic to bring interest to a dinner party. The discovery of new foods is so much fun when you can share the experience with other appreciative diners. I toasted everyone who was part of the chain in bringing the food to the table, and toasted happy, memory-making times. And I toast you cooks out there who are doing the same thing in your own way.

MAC 'N' CHEESE WITH WILD BOAR

Who doesn't love macaroni and cheese? We all do, but sometimes it just needs a little kick to jazz it up, and hearty wild boar sausage does just that. To keep this recipe from getting too wild, tame it by serving in individual cocottes.

Serves 4 to 6

For the Mac 'n' Cheese

5 cups (1.25 L) macaroni
2 tsp (10 mL) olive oil
4 wild boar sausages (about 12 oz/375 g total), casings removed, crumbled
1 tsp (5 mL) chili flakes
1 small onion, peeled and cut in half lengthwise
2 bay leaves
4 whole cloves
2 cups (500 mL) milk
3 tbsp (50 mL) unsalted butter
3 tbsp (50 mL) all-purpose flour
Salt and white pepper
2½ cups (625 mL) grated Cheddar cheese
2 tbsp (30 mL) Dijon mustard
2 tbsp (30 mL) chopped parsley

For the Topping

2 tbsp (30 mL) unsalted butter, melted
1 cup (250 mL) panko bread crumbs
¼ cup (60 mL) grated Parmesan cheese
2 tbsp (30 mL) chopped parsley

Heat your oven to 350°F (180°C). Lightly butter a 2-quart (2 L) baking dish or six 1-cup (250 mL) individual cocottes.

Cook the macaroni in boiling salted water until tender. Drain and rinse.

In a large saucepan, heat the oil over medium heat. Add the sausages and chili flakes and cook until lightly browned, about 5 minutes. Transfer to a plate and set aside.

To make the sauce, make a cut in each half of the onion about 1 inch (2.5 cm) deep, and slide a bay leaf into each slit. Stick the cloves into the onions. In a large saucepan, combine the milk and onions; heat over medium heat. Meanwhile, in a second saucepan, melt the butter over low heat. Add the flour and cook the roux, stirring, for 3 minutes. Do not let it colour. Remove from heat. Pour some hot milk into the roux, stirring until the milk is thoroughly blended in. Stir this mixture into the remaining milk and simmer, stirring frequently, for 15 minutes. Season with salt and white pepper.

Remove the onions. Add the cheese and the mustard. Continue cooking over low heat, stirring until the cheese is melted. Add the macaroni, sausage, and parsley; stir together well. Season well with salt and white pepper. Transfer to the prepared baking dish.

To make the topping, combine the melted butter, bread crumbs, Parmesan, and parsley. Sprinkle over the casserole and bake until browned and bubbly, 25 to 30 minutes.

Remove from oven and serve immediately.

Here's an idea: Italian sausage can be substituted for wild boar sausages.

WILD BOAR TENDERLOIN & BUTTERNUT SQUASH PURÉE

Wild boar is a heritage breed that's coming back in a big way. They aren't the most gorgeous of creatures, but they sure make up for it in flavour. The taste is slightly gamy while still succulent and sweet. In this recipe I turn the tenderloin into a filet mignon by wrapping it in wild boar bacon. I serve it with a much maligned vegetable, the brussels sprout, but give the little guy a makeover. By sautéing the sprout leaves in butter, you get a tender green that no one will recognize as the old mushy bowling balls of past dinners.

Serves 6 to 8

For the Wild Boar Tenderloin
8 to 10 thin slices wild boar bacon
2 wild boar tenderloins, trimmed of excess fat
1 tbsp olive oil
4 sprigs thyme
4 tbsp (50 mL) butter
¼ cup (60 mL) red wine
1 cup (250 mL) chicken stock (page 245)
2 tbsp (30 mL) chopped parsley

For the Butternut Squash Purée
1 butternut squash, cut in half lengthwise and seeded
¼ cup (60 mL) unsalted butter
2 tbsp (30 mL) maple syrup
Salt and pepper

For the Brussels Sprout Leaves
2 tbsp (30 mL) unsalted butter
1 tbsp (15 mL) finely chopped shallots
2 cups (500 mL) brussels sprouts, leaves pulled apart
Salt and pepper

For the Glazed Cipollini Onions
1 cup (250 mL) peeled and trimmed cipollini onions
¼ cup (60 mL) olive oil
1 tbsp (15 mL) thyme leaves
1 tbsp (15 mL) brown sugar
¼ cup (60 mL) sherry vinegar
¼ cup (60 mL) water
1 tbsp (15 mL) butter
Salt and pepper

To make the squash purée, preheat your oven to 375°F (190°C). Spray a large baking sheet with cooking spray. Place the squash cut side down on the prepared sheet. Bake until the squash is very tender when pierced with a fork, about 1 hour. Cool slightly. Scoop out the flesh and place it in a food processor. Pulse until smooth. Transfer the squash purée to a saucepan. Stir in the butter and maple syrup; season with salt and pepper. Gently reheat before serving.

To make the onions, preheat your oven to 375°F (190°C). Place the onions in a large ovenproof skillet with the olive oil, thyme, sugar, sherry vinegar, and water. Cover the skillet with foil and roast the onions until soft, about 20 minutes. Remove the foil and continue to roast the onions for 10 minutes. Transfer the skillet to the stovetop over medium heat. Add the butter and cook, stirring often, until the onions are richly glazed, about 2 minutes. Season with salt and pepper.

To make the wild boar tenderloin, preheat your oven to 375°F (190°C). Wrap the bacon around each tenderloin and tie it in place with butcher's twine. Heat the oil and 1 tablespoon (15 mL) of the butter in a medium ovenproof skillet over medium-high heat. Sear the tenderloins until golden brown on all sides. Add the thyme and transfer to the oven and roast for 12 to 14 minutes for medium doneness. Transfer to a cutting board and let stand 10 minutes. In the meantime, on the stove over medium-high heat, deglaze the pan with the wine and reduce until almost evaporated, about 2 minutes. Add the chicken stock and reduce by half, about 5 minutes. Whisk in the remaining butter and the parsley. Pour into a sauce boat. Remove the twine from the tenderloins and carve into thick slices.

To make the brussels sprout leaves, melt the butter in a large skillet over medium-high heat. Add the shallots and stir and cook until tender. Add the leaves and a splash of water. Sauté until the leaves are just wilted but still a bright green. Remove from heat and season with salt and pepper.

Serve this family style. Place the squash down in the centre of a large platter and top with the boar tenderloin slices. Garnish with glazed onions and brussels sprout leaves. Serve the sauce on the side.

For Dad's Meat Loaf

1 cup (250 mL) panko bread crumbs
⅓ cup (75 mL) milk
2 tbsp (30 mL) unsalted butter
1 onion, finely chopped
4 cloves garlic, minced
1 stalk celery, finely chopped
1 carrot, finely chopped
4 slices bacon, chopped
¼ cup (60 mL) ketchup
2 tsp (10 mL) Worcestershire sauce
1 tbsp (15 mL) dry mustard
1 tbsp (15 mL) finely chopped thyme
Salt and pepper
1½ lb (750 g) ground Berkshire pork
1 lb (500 g) ground beef chuck
½ lb (250 g) ground veal
2 large eggs, lightly beaten
⅓ cup (75 mL) finely chopped parsley

For the Onion Gravy

1 tbsp (15 mL) vegetable oil
1 tbsp (15 mL) unsalted butter
1 onion, thinly sliced
2 tbsp (30 mL) all-purpose flour
½ cup (125 mL) red wine
2 cups (500 mL) veal stock (page 246)
1 sprig thyme
1 bay leaf
2 tbsp (30 mL) finely chopped parsley
Salt and pepper

DAD'S MEAT LOAF

My father loved to cook.... He had some unique recipes! I say that with a big smile on my face. I loved being in the kitchen with him. He always made cooking fun. One of my favourite recipes he made for dinner was his meat loaf, and I swore it could never be improved upon—until I made it with flavourful Berkshire pork and saw that maybe a little change wasn't so bad. Soaking the bread crumbs in milk makes the final dish so moist. I suggest Japanese panko bread crumbs, as they're super light and fluffy.

Serves 6

Preheat your oven to 350°F (180°C). In a large bowl, combine the bread crumbs and milk; set aside to soak. In a large skillet over medium heat, melt the butter. Add the onions, garlic, celery, carrot, and bacon; cook, stirring occasionally, 10 minutes. Remove from heat and stir in the ketchup, Worcestershire sauce, dry mustard, and thyme; season well with salt and pepper. Add to the bread crumbs. Add the pork, beef, veal, eggs, and parsley. Gently mix with your hands. Do not over-mix.

Turn the mixture out into a 13- × 9-inch (32 × 23 cm) shallow baking dish and pack it into a 9- × 5-inch (23 × 12 cm) oval loaf. Bake until an instant-read thermometer inserted into the centre of the meat loaf registers 155°F (68°C), 1 to 1¼ hours.

To make the gravy, heat the oil and butter in a large skillet over medium-high heat. Add the onion and cook, stirring frequently, until softened and caramelized, about 15 minutes. Add the flour and cook, stirring, for 1 minute. Stir in the red wine and reduce by half. Add the stock, thyme, and bay leaf; simmer, stirring, until the gravy is slightly thickened, 8 to 10 minutes. Add the parsley and season well with salt and pepper.

To serve, slice the meatloaf into thick slices. Serve with mashed potatoes and lots of onion gravy.

IN THE
PASTURE

COWBOY-SPICED BISON CARPACCIO & SALAD

Don't be afraid to make carpaccio at home; it's super easy. This method is the most approachable I know for making beautiful, paper-thin carpaccio. A quick sear in a hot cast-iron pan and then a rest in the freezer allow the meat to firm up, making it much easier to slice.

Serves 4

12 oz (375 g) bison strip loin, trimmed
2 tbsp (30 mL) olive oil, plus more
   for brushing
2 tbsp (30 mL) Cowboy Steak Rub
   (page 259)
4 cups (1 L) loosely packed arugula
1 cup (250 mL) thinly sliced button
   mushrooms
4 radishes, thinly sliced
Salt and pepper
¼ cup (60 mL) Lemon Herb Vinaigrette
   (page 256)
Parmesan cheese for garnish
Horseradish Aïoli (page 251)

Rub the bison strip loin all over with the olive oil, then pat on the cowboy steak rub. In a cast-iron pan over high heat, sear the meat on all sides, about 1 minute per side. Transfer the bison to a plate and place in freezer to firm up for 1 hour.

Thinly slice the bison and arrange it on serving plates. Brush with some olive oil and season with salt and pepper.

In a bowl, toss the arugula, mushrooms, and radishes with the vinaigrette. Place on top of the bison carpaccio. Shave lots of Parmesan cheese on top and serve with horseradish aïoli on the side.

CREAM

What do you get when you feed the best cows the best grass all year-round? The best, most heavenly cream! Take some of that cream, simmer it gently with good vegetables, fresh spices, and great meat, and what do you have? A truly incredible dish. And simple. Or if you take that cream and just churn it for a few minutes, then what? You get the *best* butter.

I was in New Prague, Minnesota, to visit one of the finest dairy farms there is. The cows feed only on grass year-round, and what that produces is some of the sweetest, finest cream I've ever tasted, with the flavours of the meadow shining through. The connection from pasture to flavour is so direct, it's wild.

Aren't some of life's true pleasures taken from simple, good things? Bread and butter, just that, can be a perfect experience. The real joy that comes from hearty peasant-style food is the result of its straightforward combination of each fine-quality ingredient.

If you use only the best and freshest products you can find, and don't tamper with them too much, leaving each flavour to take the stage, what you get is a gorgeous whole that's greater than the sum of its parts.

SHALLOT CRÈME BRÛLÉE WITH SMOKED TROUT

I put this dish on the menu at the Four Seasons in New York and it was a huge hit—we couldn't make enough of it.

Serves 6

For the Shallot Crème Brûlée
4 cups (1 L) heavy cream
1 cup (250 mL) thinly sliced shallots
2 tbsp (30 mL) sugar
1 tsp (5 mL) salt
8 egg yolks

For the Smoked Trout Salad
1 bunch watercress
¼ cup (60 mL) Lemon Herb Vinaigrette
   (page 256)
6 oz (175 g) smoked trout
½ cup (125 mL) Pickled Kohlrabi
   (page 260)
½ small red onion, thinly sliced
1 small cucumber, seeded, halved,
   and thinly sliced

To make the crème brûlée, preheat your oven to 350°F (180°C). In a medium saucepan over medium-high heat, combine the cream, shallots, sugar, and salt. Heat the cream until it is very hot but not boiling, about 5 minutes. Remove from heat and strain. In a large bowl, whisk the egg yolks, then slowly whisk in the hot cream. Pour the mixture into 6 ramekins and place in a shallow baking dish. Carefully pour boiling water into the pan to come halfway up the sides of the ramekins. Bake until the custards are set when gently shaken, 35 to 40 minutes. Remove the custards from the water bath, cool to room temperature, and refrigerate until firm.

To make the salad, in a bowl, toss the watercress with the vinaigrette. Add the smoked trout, pickled kohlrabi, red onion, and cucumber. Toss again.

Top the crème brûlée with the salad and serve.

2 tbsp (30 mL) olive oil

1 tbsp (15 mL) unsalted butter

6 boneless skinless chicken breasts

Salt and pepper

1 small onion, finely chopped

2 cloves garlic, minced

1 cup (250 mL) quartered mushrooms

2 red bell peppers, cut into ½-inch
    (1 cm) pieces

2 tbsp (30 mL) hot paprika

2 tbsp (30 mL) sweet paprika

2 tbsp (30 mL) all-purpose flour

¼ cup (60 mL) white wine

1 cup (250 mL) chicken stock (page 245)

1 cup (250 mL) heavy cream

½ cup (125 mL) sour cream

2 tbsp (30 mL) chopped parsley

CREAMY CHICKEN PAPRIKA

This family dish is quick to assemble and full of heartwarming flavours. I learned the secret to making it from a 100-year-old Czech gentleman in New Prague, Minnesota. He told me that you must use both hot and sweet paprika, then he made me do a shot of Czech liquor called Becherovka. The paprikas I recommend, the Becherovka not so much!

Serves 6

Heat the oil and butter in a large skillet over medium-high heat. Season the chicken with salt and pepper. Sear the chicken until golden brown, about 3 minutes per side. Transfer to a plate.

Add the onions and garlic to the pan and cook, stirring, for 2 minutes. Add the mushrooms and red peppers; continue cooking for 3 to 4 minutes. Stir in the hot and sweet paprika. Season with salt and pepper. Add the flour and mix well. Deglaze the pan with the white wine and reduce until it has almost evaporated. Add the stock and heavy cream. When the liquid comes to a boil, return the chicken and its juices to the skillet. Turn down the heat to medium, and cover and cook for 12 to 15 minutes, or until the chicken is cooked through. Remove from heat and stir in the sour cream and parsley.

Serve chicken with buttered egg noodles.

GOAT CHEESE

Agassiz, British Columbia, in the heart of the Fraser Valley, is a chef's dream market: bountiful with the freshest vegetables and herbs, wonderful meats, and, my siren call, fantastic artisanal goat cheese.

If you really want to appreciate the products you're cooking with, it's vital to understand where they come from, every step of the way. The Farm House Natural Cheeses is part of a small family dairy farm located in lush green Agassiz, a farm where they raise goats and make the most amazing cheese. At Boyes Farm, I weaned a day-old baby goat, milked an entire herd, worked in the fromagerie with talented cheese maker Debra Amrein-Boyes, then wandered in awestruck amazement through acres of fresh herbs and vegetables at Claude Bouchard's organic gardens.

Made of fresh goat milk, chèvre comes in a wide variety of forms. The most common is similar to cream cheese and is slightly crumbly, creamy, and can be herbed or spiced. But it's also worth seeking out the soft farmer's cheeses and fully cured firm varieties. What I love is the taste across the board, a little tangier than cow's-milk cheese. And you know, you are what you eat. So goats that are allowed free range in the pasture create dairy products that reflect their time spent there.

1 lb (500 g) mixed young beets
    (such as red, gold, and candy cane)
½ cup (125 mL) extra-virgin olive oil
1 tsp (5 mL) salt
Leaves from 3 sprigs of thyme
2 shallots, finely chopped
3 tbsp (50 mL) white balsamic vinegar

1 tbsp (15 mL) lemon juice
Salt and pepper
2 cups (500 mL) arugula
½ cup (125 mL) parsley leaves
2 tbsp (30 mL) chopped chives
4 oz (125 g) soft mild goat cheese

ROASTED BEET & GOAT CHEESE SALAD

This classic combination is made even better when you use the best-quality goat cheese. I made this salad on a goat farm in Agassiz in British Columbia's Fraser Valley. It doesn't get any better than goat cheese made straight from the farm by Deborah Amrein-Boyes, a talented cheese maker, who raises the goats with her husband, George.

Serves 4

Preheat your oven to 425°F (220°C). Cut the greens off the beets, leaving about ½ inch (1 cm) of the stem attached. Clean the beets well and toss them with 2 tbsp (30 mL) of the olive oil, 1 tsp (5 mL) salt, and the thyme. Place the beets in a roasting pan with a splash of water in the bottom. Cover tightly with foil and roast until tender, about 45 minutes. Carefully remove the foil. Let the beets cool, then peel them by slipping off the skins with your fingers.

Slice the beets into wedges and place in a large bowl. Add the shallots. In a separate bowl, whisk together the balsamic vinegar and lemon juice. Whisk in the remaining olive oil; season with salt and pepper. Toss the beets with three-quarters of the vinaigrette. Add the arugula, parsley, and chives; toss again. Season with salt and pepper.

Divide the beets among 4 salad plates and crumble the goat cheese on top.

ROASTED EGGPLANT WITH GOAT CHEESE

I love eggplant.
Here I split and roast
it with Mediterranean
flavours and serve it
with a tomato jam and
tangy goat cheese.

Serves 4

For the Tomato Jam
½ cup (125 mL) sugar
¼ cup (60 mL) sherry vinegar
1 small white onion, chopped
2 bay leaves
4 to 5 sprigs thyme
1 vanilla bean, split lengthwise
1 tsp (5 mL) ground ginger
½ tsp (2 mL) chili flakes
2 cups (500 mL) diced tomatoes
3 tbsp (50 mL) tomato paste
Salt and black pepper

For the Eggplant and Goat Cheese
2 small eggplants, cut in half lengthwise
3 tbsp (50 mL) olive oil
8 oz (250 g) goat cheese
Leaves from 2 sprigs thyme
Salt and pepper
2 tbsp (30 mL) heavy cream
1 tsp (5 mL) finely chopped chives
1 tsp (5 mL) finely chopped parsley
1 tsp (5 mL) finely chopped chervil
2 cups (500 mL) arugula
¼ cup (60 mL) pine nuts, toasted
¼ cup (60 mL) Basil Sun-Dried Tomato
    Vinaigrette (page 257)

To make the tomato jam, in a medium saucepan over medium-high heat, melt the sugar, without stirring. As the sugar syrup begins to colour, gently swirl the pan to help it brown evenly. As soon as the caramel is a golden brown, carefully pour in the sherry vinegar. Immediately add the onions, bay leaves, thyme, vanilla bean, ginger, and chili flakes; stir well.

Add the diced tomatoes and reduce heat to medium-low. Cook, stirring frequently, until almost all the tomato juice has evaporated and the tomatoes thicken, about 20 minutes. Stir in the tomato paste and salt and pepper; cook for another 5 minutes or until no watery tomato juice is present. If using right away, remove and discard the vanilla bean, bay leaves, and thyme. If using another time, leave these in to infuse the flavour further. (The jam will keep for 2 weeks in the refrigerator.)

To roast the eggplant, preheat your oven to 375°F (190°C). Brush the eggplant generously with olive oil on both sides. Place cut side up on a baking sheet lined with parchment paper. Crumble 1 ounce (30 grams) of goat cheese on each eggplant half and sprinkle with thyme leaves, salt, and pepper. Roast until soft and golden brown, 25 to 30 minutes.

In a small bowl, whisk together the remaining goat cheese and cream until smooth. Add the chives, parsley, and chervil. Season with salt and pepper. Smear some goat cheese on a plate and place the eggplant on top. Spoon some tomato jam over the warm eggplant.

Toss the arugula and pine nuts with the vinaigrette and nestle on top of the eggplant.

GOAT RICOTTA GNOCCHI

The best way to make gnocchi is with a group. Get a bunch of people around a table and make a party out of it. Everyone will get messy, but it's always more fun to eat gnocchi when you have flour on your cheek. Soft ricotta gnocchi pillows, tossed with rich tomato basil sauce and topped with crispy prosciutto, are heaven.

Serves 4 to 6

For the Goat Ricotta Gnocchi
2 large eggs
1½ lb (750 g) goat milk ricotta, drained
1½ cups (375 mL) all-purpose flour
1 tsp (5 mL) salt
½ tsp (2 mL) pepper
¼ tsp (1 mL) nutmeg
2 cups (500 mL) Tomato Sauce
    (page 255)

For the Prosciutto Crisps
6 thin slices prosciutto

For the Garden Zucchini
3 tbsp (50 mL) extra-virgin olive oil
2 cups (500 mL) zucchini sliced ¼ inch
    (5 mm) thick
2 shallots, finely chopped
1 clove garlic, crushed
¼ cup (60 mL) finely chopped basil
Salt and pepper

To make the gnocchi, in a medium bowl, beat the eggs. Stir in the drained ricotta. Add the flour, salt, pepper, and nutmeg; stir together gently until a soft dough forms. Dust the dough, your hands, and the work surface lightly with some flour. Cut the dough into four equal pieces and set off to one side of the work surface. Place one piece of dough in front of you and pat it into a rough oblong. Using both hands, in a smooth back-and-forth motion and exerting light downward pressure, roll the dough into a rope ½ inch (1 cm) thick, flouring the dough if necessary as you roll to keep it from sticking.

Slice the ropes into 1-inch (2 cm) thick rounds. Sprinkle the rounds lightly with flour and pinch the middle of each round with your index finger and thumb. Place the gnocchi on a lightly floured baking sheet and continue forming the dough. At this point the gnocchi must be chilled for 1 hour and cooked immediately or frozen.

Meanwhile, make the prosciutto crisps. Preheat your oven to 400°F (200°C). Brush a baking sheet with olive oil, and lay the prosciutto on it in a single layer. Bake until crisp, 5 to 10 minutes. Let cool on a rack.

With 10 minutes to serve, bring a large pot of salted water to a boil.

Meanwhile, make the garden zucchini. In a large skillet, heat the olive oil over medium heat. Add the zucchini, shallots, and garlic; cook, stirring occasionally, until soft and light golden brown, 8 to 10 minutes. Remove from heat, stir in the basil, and season with salt and pepper.

Gently slip the gnocchi into the boiling water, stirring gently with a slotted spoon. Cook until the gnocchi rise to the surface, about 5 minutes. Scoop them out with the spoon onto a plate and drizzle with olive oil.

To serve, ladle the tomato sauce into 4 bowls. Top with the zucchini, then the gnocchi. Garnish each serving with a prosciutto crisp snapped in half and a drizzle of extra-virgin olive oil.

LAMB

Some people change careers a few times in their lives, some people go into the family business, and then there's Andrew Harrison of Brynog Farm in Ontario. This guy comes from a line of shepherds going back a thousand years. That's 32 generations! He's a real shepherd, and that's what I call a real family business. Take that, Don Corleone.

And you know something must've been passed on in the blood through all those generations, because this was some of the best lamb I've ever tasted—so sweet, rich, and tender. One of the biggest rewards for me in all my culinary adventures, besides the great opportunity to learn about where the food I love comes from, is the pure joy and pride I see in the farmers' faces. I saw it in spades with Andrew as he ate the lamb from his farm that I'd prepared for him.

Lamb sometimes gets a bad rap, and that's mostly because people tend to overcook it. But there's another way! In fact, there are many other ways, from basic roasted leg of lamb to exotic dishes, and guess what? Not one of them involves overcooking the lamb. Cook to a rosy-pink medium-rare and you'll really get the most from it.

LAMB TURN-OVERS & GREEK SALAD

These turnovers are what I like to call "spanokopita styled." Layered between sheets of crispy golden phyllo, the lamb is spiced with nutmeg, dill, and lots of feta cheese. Serve with a big tossed Greek salad for a perfect summer lunch in the garden.

Serves 4 to 6

For the Lamb Turnovers
½ cup (125 mL) plus 1 tbsp (15 mL) unsalted butter
2 shallots, finely chopped
2 cloves garlic, finely minced
½ lb (250 g) ground lamb
¼ cup (125 g) crumbled feta cheese
2 tbsp (30 mL) chopped parsley
2 tbsp (30 mL) chopped dill
1 tbsp (15 mL) chopped thyme
½ tsp (2 mL) freshly grated nutmeg
Salt and pepper
4 phyllo sheets
   (each 17 × 12 inches/42 × 30 cm)

For the Greek Salad
3 green onions, thinly sliced
1 cup (250 mL) finely chopped romaine hearts
1 cup (250 mL) cherry tomatoes, cut in half
¼ cup (60 mL) sliced cucumber
¼ cup (60 mL) pitted Kalamata olives
¼ lb (125 g) crumbled feta cheese
2 tbsp (30 mL) finely chopped dill
¼ cup (60 mL) olive oil
Juice of 1 lemon
Salt and pepper

To make the turnovers, preheat your oven to 375°F (190°C). In a large skillet over medium-high heat, melt 1 tbsp (15 mL) of the butter. Add the shallots and garlic; sauté until soft. Add the ground lamb and cook until no longer pink. Transfer the mixture to a bowl and cool for 5 minutes. Add the feta, parsley, dill, thyme, nutmeg, and salt and pepper. Stir well and set aside.

Melt the remaining butter, then let cool. Cover the phyllo sheets with 2 overlapping sheets of plastic wrap and a damp kitchen towel.

Arrange 1 phyllo sheet on a work surface with a long side nearest you. (Keep the remaining sheets covered.) Brush with some melted butter. Top with another phyllo sheet and brush with more butter. Cut the phyllo lengthwise into 6 strips.

Put a heaping teaspoon of lamb filling near one corner of a strip at the end nearest you. Then fold the other corner over to enclose the filling and form a triangle. Continue folding the strip, like a flag, maintaining a triangle shape. Put the turnover seam side down on a large baking sheet and brush with some melted butter. Repeat with the remaining phyllo and filling, making 12 turnovers.

Bake the turnovers until golden brown, 20 to 25 minutes. Transfer to a rack to cool slightly.

Meanwhile, in a large bowl, combine all of the salad ingredients; toss well. Season with salt and pepper. Arrange the salad onto plates and serve with lamb turnovers.

SPICED LAMB PIZZA

I first tasted a pizza like this while having lunch outside the spice market in Istanbul. Later I met a Turkish woman who showed me how to make it. It's so easy and thrillingly exotic, plus it will give you the chance to explore the vibrant flavours of new spices.

Makes two 12-inch (30 cm) pizzas

For the Pizza Dough
3 cups (750 mL) all-purpose flour
2 tsp (10 mL) active dry yeast
2 tsp (10 mL) kosher salt
1 cup (250 mL) lukewarm water
2 tbsp (30 mL) extra-virgin olive oil

For the Spiced Lamb
2 tbsp (30 mL) extra-virgin olive oil
1 large onion, finely chopped
2 garlic gloves, minced
1 lb (500 g) ground lamb
1 cup (250 mL) chopped, seeded, and peeled tomatoes
2 tbsp (30 mL) tomato paste
⅓ cup (75 mL) chopped flat-leaf parsley
¼ cup (60 mL) pine nuts, toasted
½ tsp (2 mL) salt
½ tsp (2 mL) freshly ground black pepper
¼ tsp (1 mL) chili flakes
Pinch cinnamon
Pinch ground allspice
Pinch ground cloves
1 tbsp (15 mL) lemon juice
¼ cup (60 mL) unsalted butter, melted

To make the pizza dough, in a food processor, combine the flour, yeast, and salt. While the machine is running, add the water and oil through the feed tube. Process until the dough forms a ball and is slightly sticky to the touch. If it is still dry, add another tablespoon or two of water and process for another 10 seconds.

On a floured surface, knead the dough for a few seconds to form a smooth, round ball. Put the dough in a large bowl, cover with plastic wrap, and let rise until the dough doubles in size, 1 to 2 hours.

Meanwhile, place a pizza stone in the lower third of your oven and preheat the oven to 450°F (230°C) for about an hour.

To make the filling, heat the olive oil in a large skillet over medium-high heat. Add the onions and garlic and cook, stirring frequently, until caramelized, about 10 minutes. Add the lamb, tomatoes, tomato paste, parsley, pine nuts, salt, black pepper, chili flakes, cinnamon, allspice, and cloves. Reduce heat and cook slowly, stirring occasionally, until the filling is almost dry. Remove from heat and stir in the lemon juice. Set aside.

Divide the dough in half. Shape each half into a ball. Put each ball on a lightly floured surface, sprinkle with flour, and cover with plastic wrap or a kitchen towel. Let rest for 15 minutes.

Flatten 1 ball of dough with your hands on a lightly floured surface. Starting at the centre and working outwards, use your fingertips to press the dough to ½-inch (1 cm) thickness all over. Turn and stretch the dough into a circle about 10 to 12 inches (25 to 30 cm).

To assemble the pizza, spread half the filling over each pizza, going right to the edges. Brush the filling lightly with olive oil. Bake the pizzas on the pizza stone until the crust is crisp and golden around the edges, 8 to 10 minutes.

For the Lamb and Vegetable Stew

2 lb (1 kg) boneless lamb shoulder, cut into 1-inch (2.5 cm) cubes
Salt and pepper
6 tbsp (90 mL) all-purpose flour
6 tbsp (90 mL) unsalted butter, softened
2 onions, chopped
3 cloves garlic, minced
½ cup (125 mL) white wine
2 tbsp (30 mL) tomato paste
2 cups (500 mL) veal stock (page 246)
2 tsp (10 mL) thyme leaves
2 bay leaves

4 medium leeks, white and pale green part only, cut into ½-inch (1 cm) slices
5 carrots, cut into ½-inch (1 cm) pieces
2 medium turnips, cut into ½-inch (1 cm) pieces

For the Mashed Potato Topping

2 lb (1 kg) russet potatoes, peeled and quartered
½ cup (125 mL) heavy cream
½ cup (125 mL) milk
3 tbsp (50 mL) unsalted butter
Salt and pepper

SHEPHERD'S PIE

When I spent time on a Brynog sheep farm in the Ottawa Valley, I got to know a farmer who came from a long line of shepherds, so I made this dish especially for him. How often do you get to make shepherd's pie for an actual shepherd?

Serves 6

Preheat your oven to 350°F (180°C). Season the lamb with salt and pepper. Sprinkle 3 tbsp (50 mL) of the flour over the lamb to coat. In a large ovenproof pot with a lid, melt 2 tbsp (30 mL) of the butter over medium-high heat. Brown half of the lamb, turning occasionally, about 6 minutes. With a slotted spoon, transfer the lamb to a plate. Brown the remaining lamb; transfer to the plate. Add 2 tbsp (30 mL) of the butter to the pot. Add the onions and garlic. Cook, stirring frequently, until the onions start to caramelize, 3 to 5 minutes. Add the wine and deglaze by boiling over high heat, stirring and scraping up brown bits, for about 1 minute. Stir in the tomato paste and bring to a boil. Stir until the liquid is reduced by half, about 5 minutes. Add the stock, thyme, bay leaves, browned lamb, leeks, carrots, and turnips. Stir to combine, and season with salt and pepper. Bring to a simmer over medium-high heat, and then remove from heat. Cover pot and transfer to the oven. Braise until the lamb is tender, 1½ to 2 hours.

While the lamb is cooking, make the topping. Put the potatoes in a pot of salted cold water. Bring to a simmer and cook until very tender, 20 to 25 minutes. Drain in a colander. In the same saucepan, bring the cream, milk, and butter to a simmer, until butter has melted. Force the hot potatoes through a ricer into the hot cream mixture (or mash in a bowl) and stir gently to combine. Season with salt and pepper.

Preheat the broiler. In a small bowl, stir together the remaining 2 tbsp (30 mL) butter and remaining 3 tbsp (50 mL) flour to form a paste. Spoon 1 cup (250 mL) of the cooking liquid from the pot into a small saucepan and bring to a boil. Whisk in the butter-flour mixture bit by bit, then simmer, whisking occasionally, until the sauce is thickened. Gently stir the sauce into the lamb and vegetables. Transfer the filling to a casserole dish, spoon the potatoes over the lamb filling and spread evenly. Broil about 3 inches (8 cm) from the heat until the top is golden brown, about 3 minutes.

HAY-ROASTED LAMB WITH RATATOUILLE & FRITES

Where there is local lamb, there must be hay. Ask around at the farmer's market; you might get some weird looks but I'm certain once you explain this classic farmhouse recipe, a farmer will be happy to supply you with some hay. The aroma of the wine and the hay when this is cooking is something everyone should experience at least once in their lives. For convenience, have your butcher bone and butterfly the lamb and chop the bone into pieces.

Serves 6

For the Lamb Sauce
1 lamb leg bone, cut into 2-inch (5 cm) pieces
2 carrots, cut into 1-inch (2.5 cm) pieces
2 onions, chopped
2 stalks celery, cut into 1-inch (2.5 cm) pieces
4 cloves garlic, peeled and crushed
2 tbsp (30 mL) olive oil
1½ cups (375 mL) red wine
6 cups (1.5 L) veal stock (page 246)
2 tbsp (30 mL) butter
1 tsp (5 mL) thyme leaves
1 tsp (5 mL) chopped rosemary
Salt and pepper

For the Hay-Roasted Leg of Lamb
¼ cup (60 mL) olive oil
6 cloves garlic, finely chopped
2 tbsp (30 mL) finely chopped anchovies
Zest and juice of 1 lemon
2 tbsp (30 mL) chopped capers
1 tbsp (15 mL) Dijon mustard
2 tbsp (30 mL) chopped parsley
1 tbsp (15 mL) chopped rosemary
1 tbsp (15 mL) chopped thyme
2 tbsp (30 mL) unsalted butter
2 shallots, finely chopped
8 cups (2 L) baby spinach
1 leg of lamb, 4½-5 lb (2 kg), butterflied, bones reserved for sauce
Salt and pepper
3 handfuls hay, soaked in water for 20 minutes
2 cups (500 mL) white wine (optional)

For the Ratatouille
2 tbsp (30 mL) olive oil
1 fennel bulb, cored and cut into ½-inch (1 cm) pieces
1 onion, finely chopped
2 zucchini, cut into ½-inch (1 cm) pieces
2 red bell peppers, seeded and cut into ½-inch (1 cm) pieces
1 small eggplant, cut into ½-inch (1 cm) pieces
2 cloves garlic, thinly sliced
1 tbsp (15 mL) tomato paste
2 cups (500 mL) tomato juice
¼ cup (60 mL) chopped basil
Salt and black pepper

For the Zucchini Parmesan Frites
3 medium zucchini, cut into ¼- × 2-inch (5 mm × 5 cm) sticks
1 cup (250 mL) milk
¾ cup (175 mL) all-purpose flour
¾ cup (175 mL) cornstarch
Salt and pepper
3 cups (750 mL) vegetable oil
¼ cup (60 mL) grated Parmesan cheese

To make the lamb sauce, preheat your oven to 400°F (200°C). In a roasting pan, combine the lamb bones, carrots, onions, celery, and garlic. Drizzle with the oil and toss well to coat. Roast for 1 hour, until the vegetables are well caramelized.

Place the roasting pan on top of the stove over medium-high heat. Deglaze the pan with the red wine and cook, stirring, until the wine has almost evaporated. Transfer everything to a large saucepan. Add enough stock to cover the vegetables and bones. Bring to a boil over medium-high heat, then skim off the fat. Reduce heat and simmer, uncovered, for 1 to 1½ hours. After the sauce has finished simmering, strain the sauce into a small saucepan. Bring to the sauce to a boil, then reduce heat to medium and reduce liquid to 2 cups, about ½ hour, then remove from heat and whisk in the butter, thyme, and rosemary; season with salt and pepper. Reheat the sauce before serving.

While the sauce is cooking, start preparing the leg of lamb. In a small bowl, combine half the olive oil, garlic, anchovies, lemon zest and juice, capers, mustard, parsley, rosemary, and thyme; stir to form a loose paste; set aside. In a large sauté pan over medium-high heat, melt the butter. Add the shallots and cook until they are soft. Add the spinach in batches and sauté until wilted. Season with salt and pepper. Transfer to a plate and let cool.

Preheat your oven to 450°F (230°C). Season the lamb on both sides with salt and pepper. Unfold the lamb leg and rub the marinade evenly on the inside. Spread the spinach evenly on the inside of the meat. Starting from a long side, roll the lamb into a cylinder. Tie tightly at intervals with butcher's twine.

Heat the remaining olive oil in a very large skillet over medium-high heat. Sear the lamb until brown on all sides, about 8 minutes. In a large, deep roasting pan make a layer of hay about 2 inches (5 cm) thick. Moisten the hay with the wine. Lay the lamb on the hay and cover with the rest of the hay. Place a lid on the roasting pan or seal tightly with a double layer of foil. Roast for 15 minutes, then turn the heat down to 350°F (180°C). Continue to roast the lamb until a meat thermometer inserted into the thickest part registers 135° to 140°F (58° to 60°C), about 55 minutes, depending on the size of the leg. Transfer the lamb to a platter, cover loosely with foil, and let rest for 20 minutes.

While the lamb rests, make the ratatouille. Heat the oil in a large skillet over medium heat. Add the fennel and cook, stirring occasionally, for 2 minutes. Add the onions and continue to cook until the onions are soft. Add the zucchini, peppers, eggplant, and garlic. Cook until all the vegetables are tender, about 5 minutes. Stir in the tomato paste to coat the vegetables and continue cooking for 2 minutes. Add the tomato juice and basil. Season with salt and pepper. Set aside, keeping warm.

To make the zucchini frites, in a large bowl, combine the zucchini and milk, and let sit for a few minutes. In another large bowl, combine the flour and cornstarch; season with salt and pepper. Strain the zucchini and add to flour mixture. Toss well to evenly coat. Using a sieve, remove the zucchini from the flour and shake off excess.

In a large saucepan, heat the vegetable oil over medium heat to 375°F (190°C). Working in small batches, fry the zucchini until golden brown, about 2 minutes. Transfer with a slotted spoon to paper towels to drain. Dust with Parmesan.

To serve, carve the lamb and serve with ratatouille, zucchini frites, and lamb sauce.

GRILLED LAMB SKEWERS

Everybody loves a kabob, and these were inspired by a Greek festival I attended. I like to skewer the lamb on hearty rosemary stems a few hours in advance of grilling, so they can take on that gorgeous herbaceous flavour. Serve with ouzo!

Serves 4

For the Grilled Lamb Skewers
8 sprigs rosemary (each 6 inches/10 cm) long
2 lb (1 kg) lamb sirloin, cut into 1-inch (2.5 cm) pieces
3 cloves garlic, minced
1 tbsp (15 mL) thyme leaves
2 tsp (10 mL) grated lemon zest
2 tsp (10 mL) cracked black pepper
2 tbsp (30 mL) olive oil
Grilled pita bread for serving

For the Tzatziki
1 medium cucumber, peeled, seeded, and grated
2 tsp (10 mL) salt
2 cups (500 mL) Greek-style yogurt
½ clove garlic, finely chopped
1 tbsp (15 mL) olive oil
1 tsp (5 mL) lemon juice
½ tsp (2 mL) finely chopped mint
Salt and pepper

For the Beans
1 cup (250 mL) navy beans, soaked in water overnight, drained
2 cups (500 mL) chicken stock (page 245)
2 tsp (10 mL) minced garlic
2 sprigs thyme
Juice of ½ lemon
Pinch cayenne pepper
Salt and black pepper

To start the lamb skewers, remove all the rosemary leaves from the sprigs except from the top 2 inches (5 cm). Coarsely chop the rosemary leaves. Season the lamb with the chopped rosemary, garlic, thyme, lemon zest, and pepper. Cover and refrigerate for 2 hours.

To make the tzatziki, in a medium bowl, toss the grated cucumber with the salt; set aside for 20 minutes. Squeeze the cucumber to release as much liquid as possible. Return the cucumber to the bowl and stir in the yogurt, garlic, olive oil, lemon juice, and mint. Season with salt and pepper. Chill until needed.

To make the beans, in a large saucepan, combine the beans, chicken stock, garlic, and thyme sprigs. Bring to a boil, then reduce heat to a simmer. Cook, uncovered, until the beans are soft, 25 to 30 minutes. Drain the beans, reserving any liquid; discard the thyme sprigs. Place the beans in a food processor and purée. With the motor running, slowly pour in some of the reserved cooking liquid until the mixture is smooth. Season with lemon juice, cayenne, and salt and pepper. Set aside, keeping warm.

To finish the lamb skewers, preheat your grill to medium-high. Skewer 3 or 4 pieces of lamb on each rosemary sprig. Brush the lamb with the olive oil. Grill for 3 minutes on each side, rotating the skewers a few times to get even colour.

To serve, spoon the warm bean purée onto a warm platter and arrange the skewers on top. Spoon some of the tzatziki over the lamb. Serve with grilled pita bread.

4 bison rib-eye steaks (each 8 oz/250 g)
Salt and pepper
2 tbsp (60 mL) olive oil
6 tbsp (90 mL) unsalted butter
2 sprigs thyme
½ cup (125 mL) pearl onions, peeled
2 cups (500 mL) quartered button
    mushrooms

¼ cup (60 mL) vegetable stock
    (page 247)
1 cup (250 mL) cherry tomatoes,
    cut in half
2 bunches asparagus, peeled and cut
    diagonally into 1-inch (2.5 cm) pieces
2 tbsp (30 mL) chopped parsley

BISON RIB-EYE STEAKS

When I fed bison ranchers and wranglers in Airdrie, Alberta, I figured if I was going to give a cowboy a steak, I'd better give him a rib-eye. Basting the rib-eyes in thyme-scented butter and plating them with bourguignon trimmings like pearl onions and button mushrooms help to elevate the dish from chuckwagon status.

Serves 4

Heat a cast-iron skillet over medium-high heat. Season the steaks with salt and pepper. Add 1 tbsp (15 mL) of the olive oil to the pan, then add 2 of the steaks. Sear on each side for 3 to 4 minutes for medium-rare. Add 2 tbsp (30 mL) of the butter and a sprig of thyme to the pan and baste the steaks on both sides with the foaming butter. Transfer the steaks to a plate, cover loosely with foil, and pour out excess butter. Repeat with the remaining 2 steaks. Let the steaks rest for 5 minutes before serving.

Melt 2 tbsp (30 mL) of the butter in a large sauté pan over medium-high heat. Add the pearl onions and cook, stirring frequently, until the onions begin to caramelize. Add the mushrooms and sauté together for 5 minutes or until the mushrooms are cooked. Add the vegetable stock, tomatoes, asparagus, and parsley; continue cooking for 2 minutes. Remove from heat and season with salt and pepper.

To serve, place the steaks in the middle of 4 large dinner plates. Top with the mushroom mixture.

BISON

I went to Big Sky country and stood in the shadows of Alberta's Rocky Mountains, and I got my my bison on. Yeehaw! What an amazing creature. I've never seen an animal that's so imposing. The bison is truly a fantastically scary animal.

Before the great slaughter that almost wiped out the species, there were an estimated 70 million roaming the great plains of North America. Today, thanks to our bison ranchers, that herd is once again growing strong. It's largely the enjoyment of bison meat that has allowed the species to survive, so come on, do your duty as a preservationist: EAT!

But really, the main reason to cook and enjoy bison is its taste and quality, and they go hand in hand. Bison isn't gamey. It tastes like meat—real red meat, full of flavour. It's good and good for you. Bison is low in cholesterol, low in fat, and high in vitamins and minerals.

The cuts of meat will be familiar since they're the same as beef. And I predict, down the road, bison will once again become a North American staple. As with lamb, just watch that you don't overcook it. From carpaccio to pot roast, you can strut your culinary stuff with bison and do just about anything with it.

BISON SHORT RIBS

Braised short ribs are probably my favourite things to make for friends. A braise is simply a way of slowly cooking something, usually a tougher cut of meat, at a lower-than-normal temperature. The braising liquid is enriched by the smoky bacon, caramelized vegetables, herbs, wine, and rich espresso flavour. The ribs are so tender that they melt in your mouth. Luxurious, spicy, smoky, tender bison!

Serves 4

For the Coffee-Braised Short Ribs
4 lb (2 kg) bison short ribs
2 tbsp (30 mL) Cowboy Steak Rub
    (page 259)
2 tbsp (30 mL) ground espresso coffee
3 tbsp (50 mL) olive oil
2 slices bacon, diced
1 onion, cut into 1-inch (2.5 cm) pieces
8 cloves garlic, peeled and cut in half
4 shallots, chopped
2 carrots, cut into 1-inch (2.5 cm) pieces
2 stalks celery, chopped
2 tbsp (30 mL) tomato paste
2 cups (500 mL) red wine
2 sprigs thyme
2 sprigs rosemary
2 bay leaves
6 cups (1.5 L) beef stock
Salt and pepper

For the Garlic-Thyme Brown Butter
¼ cup (60 mL) unsalted butter
1 tbsp (15 mL) chopped garlic
2 tsp (10 mL) chopped rosemary
2 tsp (10 mL) chopped parsley
1 tsp (5 mL) grated lemon zest
Salt and pepper

To make the short ribs, preheat your oven to 350°F (180°C). Rub the short ribs with the steak rub and espresso. In a large, ovenproof Dutch oven over medium-high heat, heat the oil. Add the short ribs and brown them on all sides, about 8 minutes. Transfer to a plate. Add the bacon and cook until bacon is half-cooked. Add the onions, garlic, shallots, carrots, and celery. Reduce heat to medium and cook, stirring occasionally, until the vegetables are soft, about 10 minutes. Stir in the tomato paste and red wine, scraping up the browned bits. Add the thyme, rosemary, bay leaves, and stock; bring to a boil. Return the ribs and any juices to the pot, cover, and transfer to the oven. Braise until the meat is tender, 2½ to 3 hours.

Remove the ribs from the pot. Strain the braising liquid into a medium saucepan. Over medium heat, reduce the liquid until the sauce thickens.

Meanwhile, make the brown butter sauce. In a small saucepan over medium heat, melt the butter, then add the garlic and cook, stirring, until the garlic becomes golden brown. Remove from heat and stir in the rosemary, parsley, and lemon zest. Season with salt and pepper.

Transfer the ribs and sauce to a serving bowl. Drizzle the butter over the ribs.

SWEETS

CHOCOLATE PECAN TART

While in Texas, I enjoyed one of the best pecan pies I have ever eaten. This recipe was inspired by my time there cooking with Tracy. This delicious recipe is easy to make, especially the crust, and the chocolate adds so much to the sweet nuttiness of the toasted pecans.

Serves 10

For the Crust
1¼ cups (300 mL) all-purpose flour
3 tbsp (50 mL) packed golden
   brown sugar
½ tsp (2 mL) salt
½ cup (125 mL) melted unsalted butter

For the Filling
1 cup (250 mL) packed golden
   brown sugar
3 large eggs
2 tbsp (30 mL) bourbon
3 tbsp (50 mL) melted unsalted butter
¼ tsp (1 mL) salt
1¾ cups (425 mL) pecan halves and
   pieces, toasted
4 ounces (125 g) chopped semi-sweet
   chocolate

For the Sweet Vanilla Whipped Cream
1 cup (250 mL) heavy cream
2 tbsp (30 mL) sugar
½ tsp (2 mL) vanilla extract, or seeds
   from ½ vanilla bean

To make the crust, preheat your oven to 375°F (190°C). Butter a 9-inch (23 cm) round tart pan with removable bottom. In a medium bowl, whisk the flour, brown sugar, and salt to blend. Add the melted butter and stir with a fork until moist clumps form. Break into small pieces and scatter over the bottom of the pan. Using your fingertips, press the dough evenly onto the bottom and up the sides of the pan. Bake the crust until just golden brown, about 15 minutes.

Meanwhile, make the filling. In a large bowl, beat the brown sugar, eggs, bourbon, butter, and salt until well blended. Stir in the pecans and chocolate. Pour the filling into the crust and bake the tart for about 25 minutes, until just set. Remove from oven and let cool completely.

Just before serving, make the sweet vanilla whipped cream. In a large bowl, whisk the cream, sugar, and vanilla until soft peaks form. The cream should hold its shape but still be satiny in appearance.

Cut tart into wedges and serve with sweet vanilla whipped cream.

For the Pecan Biscuit Topping

1 cup (250 mL) all-purpose flour

⅔ cup (150 mL) medium-grind cornmeal

¼ cup (60 mL) plus 3 tbsp (50 mL) sugar

2 tsp (10 mL) baking powder

½ tsp (2 mL) coarse kosher salt

6 tbsp (90 mL) cold unsalted butter, cut into ½-inch (1 cm) cubes

⅔ cup (150 mL) heavy cream

3 tbsp (50 mL) unsalted butter, melted

For the Pecan Blueberry Filling

6 cups (1.5 L) fresh blueberries

1½ cups (375 mL) sugar

½ cup (125 mL) all-purpose flour

⅓ cup (75 mL) water

2 tbsp (30 mL) lemon juice

1 tsp (5 mL) vanilla extract

½ tsp (2 mL) cinnamon

For the Lemon Sabayon

6 egg yolks

1 cup (250 mL) Marsala or other dessert wine

⅓ cup (75 mL) sugar

2 tbsp (30 mL) lemon juice

PECAN BLUEBERRY COBBLER

I came up with this recipe in North Carolina after spending some quality time lounging under a pecan tree. Those pecans ended up in the cobbler dough, adding their rich nuttiness to this classic American dessert. Wild blueberries are fantastic since they have such a tart spice you can't find in domesticated berries. I finished by garnishing the cobbler with a creamy tart lemon sabayon.

Serves 6 to 8

To make the topping, in a large bowl whisk together the flour, cornmeal, ¼ cup (60 mL) of the sugar, baking powder, and salt. Add the cubed butter and rub it in with your fingertips until the mixture resembles coarse meal. Add the cream and stir until moistened. Gather the dough together and shape it into an 8-inch (20 cm) log. Cut the log crosswise into eight 1-inch (2.5 cm) thick rounds. Spread 3 tbsp (50 mL) of the sugar on a plate. Dip 1 cut side of each biscuit into the melted butter, then dip the buttered side in the sugar. Place biscuits sugared side up on a platter; sprinkle with any remaining sugar. Cover and chill for about 30 minutes.

Meanwhile, preheat your oven to 425°F (220°F). Lightly grease an 8-inch (20 cm) square baking dish.

To make the blueberry filling, combine the blueberries, sugar, flour, water, lemon juice, vanilla, and cinnamon in a saucepan. Stir over medium-high heat until the sugar melts, then reduce heat to low and cook for 10 minutes until filling thickens slightly.

Spoon the blueberry filling into the baking dish. Place the biscuits sugared side up on top of the blueberries and bake the cobbler for 15 minutes.

To make the sabayon, bring a medium saucepan of water to a gentle boil. In a stainless-steel bowl, whisk together the yolks, wine, and sugar. Set the bowl over the saucepan. Whisk constantly for 4 to 5 minutes or more to cook the sauce, until it has the consistency of lightly whipped cream. Whisk in lemon juice. When thick, foamy, and tripled in volume, remove the sabayon from heat. Serve immediately over the warm cobbler.

CHOCOLATE CHERRY SHORT-CAKES

I get so excited every year when the cherry blossoms come out, and while they are beautiful, I'm really just waiting for them to drop and give me some shiny new cherries to pick.

Here I take a wonderful shortcake recipe and add Dutch cocoa, semi-sweet chocolate, and crimson cherries, making a richer, more luxurious dessert.

Makes 8 shortcakes

For the Chocolate Cherry Shortcakes
2 cups (500 mL) all-purpose flour
½ cup (125 mL) Dutch-process
    cocoa powder
1 tbsp (15 mL) baking powder
1 tsp (5 mL) salt
½ cup (125 mL) sugar plus more for
    dipping
1 cup (250 mL) dried cherries
1 cup (250 mL) semi-sweet
    chocolate chips
2 cups (500 mL) heavy cream
6 tbsp (90 mL) unsalted butter, melted
Icing sugar for dusting

For the Cherries Jubilee
⅔ cup (150 mL) sugar
1 vanilla bean, split lengthwise
¾ cup (175 mL) water
3 cups (750 mL) pitted red cherries
2 tbsp (30 mL) cornstarch
Sweet Vanilla Whipped Cream
    (page 216)

To make the shortcakes, preheat your oven to 400°F (200°C). In a large bowl, stir together the flour, cocoa, baking powder, salt, and ½ cup (125 mL) of the sugar. Stir in the dried cherries and chocolate chips. Add the cream and stir until the mixture becomes a stiff dough. Turn out onto a work surface and use your hands to press the dough into a square about 2 inches (5 cm) thick. Cut this dough into 8 squares. Spread some additional sugar in a shallow dish. Dip the top of each square into the melted butter and then into the sugar, pressing lightly so it adheres. On an ungreased baking sheet, place the shortcakes sugared side up 2 inches (5 cm) apart. Bake for 15 minutes until they have risen. An inserted skewer should come out clean. Let cool completely on the pan.

While the shortcakes cool, make the cherries jubilee. In a large saucepan, bring the sugar, vanilla bean, and water to a boil, stirring so sugar dissolves. Reduce heat to medium and simmer for 3 minutes. Add the cherries and bring the mixture to a simmer. In a small bowl, stir together the cornstarch and 2 tbsp (30 mL) cold water. Stir into the cherry mixture and cook, stirring, for 1 minute or until thickened. Remove from heat.

To serve, cut the shortcakes in half lengthwise. Divide the sweet vanilla whipped cream among the bottom halves. Spoon the cherries jubilee over the cream, then top with the shortcake tops. Dust with icing sugar.

CHOCOLATE PEANUT BUTTER LAYER CAKE

The Eastern Shore has had a love affair with cakes from the early days of Chesapeake heritage. The Smith Island cake is Maryland's official dessert. This decadent cake has been known as "Frosting with the Cake," containing 6 to 12 pencil-thin yellow cake layers with rich chocolate fudge icing in between! Imagine this version, with nine of the most delicate layers of spongy yellow cake separated by the thinnest layers of chocolate icing and peanut butter cups!

Serves 10

For the Vanilla Sponge Cake
3 cups (750 mL) cake-and-pastry flour
1 tbsp (15 mL) baking powder
½ tsp (2 mL) salt
1 cup (250 mL) unsalted butter,
    at room temperature
2 cups (500 mL) sugar
5 large eggs
2 tsp (10 mL) vanilla extract
1¼ cups (300 mL) buttermilk
10 large chocolate peanut butter cups

For the Chocolate Frosting
⅔ cup (150 mL) milk
3 large egg yolks
1 tbsp (15 mL) plus 1 tsp (5 mL)
    all-purpose flour
1⅓ cups (325 mL) icing sugar
Pinch of salt
1 tsp (5 mL) vanilla
1½ cups (375 mL) unsalted butter,
    cut into 2-tbsp (30 mL) pieces
    and softened
8 oz (250 g) milk chocolate, melted and cooled
2 oz (60 g) unsweetened chocolate, melted
    and cooled

To make the cake, preheat your oven to 350°F (180°C). Grease four 8-inch (20 cm) round cake pans with cooking spray, dust with half of the flour, and knock out any excess; reserve the excess.

In a medium bowl, sift together all the flour, the baking powder, and salt. In the bowl of a mixer fitted with the paddle attachment, beat the butter on medium-high speed for 3 minutes, until the butter is light and creamy in colour. Add the sugar, ¼ cup (60 mL) at a time, beating for about 1 minute after each addition. Scrape the sides of the bowl occasionally. Add the eggs 1 at a time, beating well after each addition. Stir the vanilla into the buttermilk. Reduce the speed and add the dry ingredients alternately with the buttermilk in two additions. Mix just until incorporated.

Divide the batter among the prepared cake pans. Using the back of a spoon, spread the batter so that it covers the bottom of each pan, making it slightly higher around the edges than in the middle. Bake until cooked through and golden around the edges, 12 to 14 minutes. Let cool slightly, then loosen cake layers with a knife and invert onto racks. Cool completely.

In a food processor, pulse 4 peanut butter cups into small chunks; transfer to a small bowl. Pulse the remaining peanut butter cups into a fine powder; transfer to another small bowl. Chill both until ready to use.

To make the frosting, bring the milk to a simmer in a large saucepan over medium heat. In a bowl, whisk together the yolks, flour, ⅓ cup (75 mL) of the icing sugar, and a pinch of salt. Add the hot milk in a stream, whisking constantly. Return the mixture to the saucepan and bring to a boil, whisking, over medium heat. Whisk until very thick, about 3 minutes. Transfer to the bowl of a mixer. Cover surface of custard with a buttered round of waxed paper. Cool completely at room temperature, about 45 minutes.

Add vanilla and remaining 1 cup (250 mL) of icing sugar to the custard. Beat at medium speed until well combined. Increase speed to medium-high and beat in the butter, one piece at a time, until smooth. Add the chocolates and beat until combined well.

Cut each cake in half horizontally, so that you have 8 layers. Place the first layer on a serving plate. Spread with about 3 tbsp (50 mL) of frosting, then sprinkle with about 1 tbsp (15 mL) of the powdered peanut butter cups. Top with another cake layer and repeat the process to make 8 layers in all. Frost the top and sides of the cake with the remaining icing. Sprinkle the top with the peanut butter cup chunks.

VANILLA RICE PUDDING

This creamy stovetop rice pudding can be served hot or cold and will satisfy your sweet dessert cravings. What makes this comfort food classic so special are the oranges! Candied oranges and a delightful, elegant sabayon.

Serves 8

For the Vanilla Rice Pudding
1 cup (250 mL) arborio rice
1¾ cups (425 mL) water
1 cup (250 mL) milk
½ cup (125 mL) sugar
½ vanilla bean, split lengthwise, seeds scraped
¼ tsp (1 mL) salt
1 cup (250 mL) heavy cream

For the Candied Oranges
3 oranges, unpeeled, very thinly sliced
2 cups (500 mL) water
1½ cups (375 mL) honey
½ cup (125 mL) sugar

For the Orange Sabayon
5 large egg yolks
⅓ cup (75 mL) sugar
Pinch of salt
1 cup (250 mL) Muscat or late-harvest Riesling
¾ cup (175 mL) heavy cream
2 tsp (10 mL) freshly squeezed orange juice

In a medium saucepan combine the rice, water, milk, sugar, vanilla bean and seeds, and salt. Bring to a boil, then reduce heat and simmer until the rice has absorbed almost all the liquid, 18 to 20 minutes. Remove from heat and stir until smooth. Remove the vanilla bean. Let cool slightly.

Bring a large pot of water to a boil. Add the orange slices and cook until translucent, about 5 minutes. Transfer to a baking sheet. Cut a piece of parchment into a circle to fit a large, shallow saucepan. In the saucepan, bring the water, honey, and sugar to a boil. Add the orange slices and place the parchment directly on top. Reduce heat and simmer until the oranges are soft and the liquid has reduced to syrup, about 45 minutes. Remove from heat and let cool.

Fill a medium saucepan with 2 inches (5 cm) of water and set over medium heat to bring to a simmer. In a large stainless-steel bowl, whisk together the egg yolks, sugar, and salt until very pale yellow. Whisk in the wine. Place the bowl over the pan of simmering water, and whisk until the mixture has thickened and tripled in volume, 5 to 10 minutes. Set the bowl inside a large bowl of ice and ice water. Whisk until cooled, about 5 minutes. In a large bowl whip the heavy cream until soft peaks form. Whisk in the orange juice. Fold into the cooled sabayon.

To finish the rice pudding, whip the heavy cream until soft peaks form. Fold into the rice pudding. Divide pudding among serving dishes. Top with the oranges slices and syrup. Finish with the orange sabayon.

GREEN TEA POACHED PEARS

Making a dessert cannot get easier than this. Pears slowly simmered in sweet green tea with vanilla and orange are turned into little jewels. They have a wonderful creamy and rich mascarpone centre and are decorated with a crisp, golden pistachio brittle.

Serves 4

For the Pistachio Brittle
¼ cup (60 mL) sugar
1 tbsp (15 mL) honey
1 tbsp (15 mL) pistachios, finely chopped
¼ tsp (1 mL) sea salt

For the Green Tea Poached Pears
6 bags green tea
1 cup (250 mL) dark brown sugar
1-inch (2.5 cm) piece ginger, peeled and thinly sliced
1 orange, thinly sliced
1 vanilla bean, split lengthwise and seeds scraped
4 Bosc pears, peeled and cored but kept whole
½ cup (125 mL) mascarpone cheese
¼ cup (60 mL) granulated sugar
½ tsp (2 mL) vanilla extract
Zest and juice of 1 orange

To make the pistachio brittle, spray a baking sheet with vegetable cooking spray. In a small saucepan, combine the sugar, honey, and 2 tbsp (30 mL) water. Bring to a boil, without stirring, over medium-high heat and cook until deep golden brown, 4 to 5 minutes. Pour onto the prepared baking sheet and tilt the sheet so the caramel spreads thinly. Immediately sprinkle evenly with the pistachios and salt. Let cool completely, then break into large pieces. This step can be done ahead of time and the brittle stored at room temperature in an airtight container.

To poach the pears, cut a circle of parchment paper the same diameter as a large saucepan. Bring 4 cups (1 L) of water to a boil in the saucepan. Add the tea bags, remove from heat, and let steep for 10 minutes. Remove the tea bags. Add the brown sugar, ginger, orange slices, and vanilla seeds and bean. Bring to a simmer over medium-high heat, and simmer for 5 minutes. Add the pears and reduce heat to a gentle simmer. Cover the pears with the parchment circle to keep them submerged. Poach until just tender, about 20 minutes. Using a slotted spoon, remove the pears and chill. Strain the liquid, return it to the saucepan, and boil until reduced to 1 cup (250 mL), about 30 minutes, then chill.

To make the pear stuffing, combine the mascarpone cheese, granulated sugar, vanilla, and orange zest and juice; stir together well. Using a piping bag, stuff the pears with the mascarpone.

To serve, stand a pear in each bowl and ladle the green tea sauce around them. Garnish with the pistachio brittle.

CRAN-BERRY FRUIT STEW

When I was a kid, baked apples with brown sugar were one of my favourite things. I decided to update that old standby and stuff them with an autumnal fruit stew that uses orchard fruits and cranberries. The tart cranberry really shines here. Once each apple is stuffed, top with granola and serve as a warm dessert after dinner or as a delightful course at brunch.

Serves 6

For the Baked Apple Cups

6 apples, Gala or Cortland, tops cut off and hollowed out, leaving a ½-inch (1 cm) shell
3 tbsp (50 mL) unsalted butter, softened
2 tbsp (30 mL) dark brown sugar

For the Fruit Stew

¼ cup (60 mL) unsalted butter
2 apples, cored and diced
2 pears, cored and diced
2 plums, diced
2 peaches, diced
¼ cup (60 mL) fresh or frozen cranberries
¼ cup (60 mL) sun-dried cranberries
½ cup (125 mL) dark brown sugar
1 vanilla bean, split
1 cup (250 mL) cranberry juice
1 banana, cut into 1-inch (2.5 cm) slices
2 cups (500 mL) granola

Preheat your oven to 350°F (180°C).

To make the baked apple cups, brush the insides of the hollowed-out apples with the soft butter, then coat with the brown sugar. Place on a baking sheet and bake for 20 minutes or until just soft to the touch. Let cool for 10 minutes before filling with the fruit stew.

To make the fruit stew, in a large saucepan, melt the butter over medium-high heat. Add the apples, pears, plums, peaches, fresh and dried cranberries, brown sugar, and vanilla bean. Cook for 5 minutes, stirring occasionally. Add the cranberry juice. Reduce heat and simmer for 15 to 20 minutes, or until the fruit is soft. Remove from heat and remove the vanilla bean. Stir in the banana.

Fill each of the apple cups with the fruit mixture, then top with granola. Bake for 10 minutes.

1 cup (250 mL) unsalted butter

1 cup (250 mL) firmly packed dark brown sugar

2 cups (500 mL) fresh cranberries

¼ cup (60 mL) sun-dried cranberries

¾ cup (175 mL) coarsely chopped walnuts, toasted

3 large eggs

1 cup (250 mL) canned pumpkin purée

6 tbsp (90 mL) vegetable oil

1½ cups (375 mL) all-purpose flour

1 cup (250 mL) sugar

1½ tsp (7 mL) baking powder

1 tsp (5 mL) cinnamon

¼ tsp (1 mL) salt

Sweet Vanilla Whipped Cream (page 216)

CRAN-BERRY WALNUT PUMPKIN UPSIDE-DOWN CAKE

Preheat your oven to 350°F (180°C). Line the bottom of a 9-inch (23 cm) square cake pan with parchment paper.

Melt the butter in a small saucepan over medium heat. Add the brown sugar and whisk until smooth. Pour the mixture into the cake pan. Combine the fresh cranberries, sun-dried cranberries, and walnuts. Spread them over the brown sugar mixture.

In a large bowl, whisk together the eggs, pumpkin purée, and oil. In a medium bowl, sift together the flour, sugar, baking powder, cinnamon, and salt. Stir the flour mixture into the pumpkin mixture until combined. Carefully spread the batter over the cranberry walnut topping.

Bake until a tester inserted in the middle comes out clean, 35 to 40 minutes. Cool the cake for 10 minutes on a rack. Place a large plate or platter on top of the cake. Invert the cake and plate together. Remove the pan. Carefully peel off the parchment paper.

Serve with sweet vanilla whipped cream.

When I was in Plymouth, Massachusetts, I had an upside-down cake similar to this one; it reminds me of the East Coast in the fall. Once you taste it, you'll wonder why pumpkins and cranberries don't hang out more often.

Serves 8 to 10

RED VELVET CUPCAKES

Everyone seems to enjoy red velvet cupcakes covered with lovely swirls of cream cheese frosting. Hands down, these are my favourite cupcake on the planet. I could seriously eat one of these a day and never get tired of them.

Makes 12 cupcakes

For the Red Velvet Cupcakes

1¼ cups (300 mL) sifted cake-and-pastry flour
2 tbsp (50 mL) Dutch-processed cocoa powder
¼ tsp (1 mL) baking powder
½ tsp (2 mL) baking soda
¼ tsp (1 mL) salt
½ cup (125 mL) buttermilk
1 tbsp (15 mL) red food colouring
1 tsp (5 mL) vanilla extract
½ tsp (2 mL) distilled white vinegar
¾ cup (200 mL) sugar
¼ cup (60 mL) unsalted butter, at room temperature
1 large egg
2 cups (500 mL) fresh berries for garnish

For the Cream Cheese Frosting

1 pkg (8 oz/250 g) cream cheese, at room temperature
½ tsp (2 mL) vanilla extract
½ cup (125 mL) icing sugar
⅔ cup (150 mL) heavy cream

To make the cupcakes, preheat your oven to 350°F (180°C). Line a 12-cup muffin pan with paper liners. In a medium bowl, sift the sifted flour, cocoa, baking powder, baking soda, and salt. In a small bowl, whisk together the buttermilk, food colouring, vanilla, and vinegar. In the bowl of a mixer, beat the sugar with the butter until well blended. Add the egg and beat together. Add the dry ingredients in 4 additions alternately with the buttermilk mixture in 3 additions.

Fill muffin cups two-thirds full. Bake for 20 to 22 minutes, turning the pans once halfway through, until a toothpick inserted in the centre comes out clean. Cool completely before frosting.

To make the frosting, in a large bowl, beat the cream cheese until smooth. Add the vanilla and icing sugar and beat until smooth. Using a whisk attachment, gradually add the heavy cream and whip until the frosting is thick enough to pipe.

Frost the cupcakes with a butter knife or pipe it on with a large star tip. Garnish with fresh berries.

WARM PEAR CAKE WITH BACON CARAMEL SAUCE

This is one of our signature desserts at Ruby Watchco. Did I mention that I'm obsessed with wild boar bacon? The evidence is right here in this dessert. The Bartlett pears are caramelized and then topped with a sour cream cake batter. The warm boar-bacon-studded caramel is the salty sweet drizzle that ensures there will be no leftovers.

Makes 6 cakes

For the Caramelized Pears
3 tbsp (50 mL) unsalted butter
4 Bartlett pears, peeled, cored, and diced
1 tbsp (15 mL) sugar
1 tbsp (15 mL) lemon juice

For the Sour Cream Cakes
1½ cups (375 mL) all-purpose flour
1½ tsp (7 mL) baking powder
¾ tsp (4 mL) salt
½ cup (125 mL) unsalted butter, at room temperature
⅔ cup (150 mL) sugar
2 large eggs
1½ tsp (7 mL) vanilla extract
½ cup (125 mL) sour cream

For the Wild Boar Bacon Caramel Sauce
¾ cup (175 mL) sugar
¾ cup (175 mL) heavy cream
⅛ tsp (0.5 mL) salt
8 slices wild boar bacon, diced and cooked until crisp

To make the caramelized pears, melt the butter in a large saucepan over medium-high heat. When the foam subsides, add the pears and sauté until just beginning to brown, 2 to 3 minutes. Stir in the sugar and lemon juice. Increase heat to high and cook, stirring, until the juices are deep golden and the pears are tender, about 5 minutes. Set aside.

To make the sour cream cakes, preheat your oven to 375°F (190°C). Coat 6 ramekins with vegetable cooking spray. In a medium bowl, combine the flour, baking powder, and salt. In the bowl of a mixer, beat the butter until smooth. Gradually add the sugar, beating until well blended. Add the eggs and vanilla; beat until blended. Beat in the flour mixture, then the sour cream. Place 1 tbsp (15 mL) of the caramelized pears in each of the ramekins, then cover with the cake batter. Bake for 20 to 25 minutes, until golden brown and a tester inserted into the centre comes out clean.

While the cakes are baking, make the caramel sauce. In a large, heavy saucepan over medium-high heat, bring the sugar and ¼ cup (60 mL) of water to a boil. Cook, swirling the pan occasionally, until the sugar syrup is light golden brown, 6 to 8 minutes. Remove from heat, then carefully stir in the cream. (The caramel sauce will boil rapidly when you first add the cream.) Stir in the salt and bacon. Return to heat and bring to a boil, stirring until smooth. Remove from heat and keep the sauce warm.

To serve, unmould the cakes onto plates and drizzle with warm caramel sauce.

½ cup (125 mL) unsalted butter, softened, plus 3 tbsp (50 mL) for pan
1 cup (250 mL) plus 2 tbsp (30 mL) sugar
3 ripe peaches (1 lb/500 g), skins on, pitted and cut into ¾-inch (2 cm) wedges
1 cup (250 mL) yellow cornmeal

¾ cup (175 mL) all-purpose flour
1 tsp (5 mL) baking powder
1¼ tsp (6 mL) coarse salt
3 large eggs
½ tsp (2 mL) vanilla extract
1½ cups (375 mL) heavy cream
2 tbsp (30 mL) bourbon

PEACH UPSIDE-DOWN CORNCAKE

This cake reminds me of eating peaches in the Georgia sunshine and drinking a mint julep from a mason jar. It's a moist corn cake baked in a skillet and served up with bourbon whipped cream, a perfect southern dessert.

Serves 8

Preheat your oven to 350°F (180°C). In a 10-inch (25 cm) cast-iron skillet over medium heat, melt 3 tbsp (50 mL) of the butter, using a pastry brush to coat the sides with the butter. Sprinkle ¼ cup (60 mL) of the sugar evenly over the bottom of the skillet, and cook, without stirring, until the sugar starts to bubble and turns golden brown, about 3 minutes. Arrange the peaches in a circle around the outside edge of the skillet, then in smaller circles to fill the skillet. Reduce heat and cook until the peaches begin to soften, 10 minutes. Remove from heat.

Combine the cornmeal, flour, baking powder, and salt. In the bowl of a mixer, beat ½ cup (125 mL) of the butter and ¾ cup (175 mL) of the sugar until pale and fluffy, about 3 minutes. Add the eggs, 1 at a time, beating well after each addition and scraping down the sides of the bowl. Beat in the vanilla and ½ cup (125 mL) of the heavy cream. Reduce speed to low and beat in the cornmeal mixture.

Drop large spoonfuls of the batter over the peaches, then spread evenly. Bake until golden brown and a tester inserted in the centre comes out clean, 20 to 25 minutes. Transfer skillet to a rack and let stand for 10 minutes. Invert the cake onto a platter. Let cool slightly before serving.

In a bowl, beat the remaining 1 cup (250 mL) heavy cream, the remaining 2 tbsp (30 mL) sugar, and the bourbon until soft peaks form. Serve on top of the cake.

FLOATING ISLANDS WITH CLOUD-BERRIES

A meringue poached in sweet milk and plated on a pool of crème anglaise flecked with fresh vanilla is a French classic, but this dessert needed something to make it sing. Sugared cloudberries did just the trick and turned this island into Shangri-La.

Serves 4 to 6

For the Sugared Cloudberries
1 cup (250 mL) cloudberries
½ cup (125 mL) sugar
1 vanilla bean, split lengthwise

For the Cloudberry Crème Anglaise
2 cups (500 mL) heavy cream
½ cup (125 mL) sugar
1 vanilla bean, split lengthwise
4 egg yolks
¼ cup (60 mL) cloudberries

For the Floating Islands
2 cups (500 mL) milk
8 egg whites
¼ tsp (1 mL) salt
1 cup (250 mL) sugar
1 tsp (5 mL) vanilla extract

To make the sugared cloudberries, toss the cloudberries with the sugar and vanilla bean. Transfer to a mason jar and refrigerate overnight.

To make the crème anglaise, in a saucepan, heat the cream, half of the sugar, and the vanilla bean over medium heat. In a bowl, whisk together the egg yolks and remaining sugar until thick and pale. Whisk in the hot cream in a thin stream. Pour back into the saucepan and add the cloudberries. Cook over medium heat, stirring constantly, until thick enough to coat the back of a spoon, 2 to 3 minutes. Strain to remove the cloudberry seeds and vanilla, pour into a clean bowl, and chill.

Make the floating islands just before serving. Bring the milk to a simmer in a large sauté pan over medium heat. Reduce heat to medium-low.

In the bowl of a mixer fitted with the whisk attachment, beat the egg whites with the salt on medium speed until frothy. Turn the mixer to high speed and add the sugar, 1 tbsp (15 mL) at a time. Beat until the egg whites are very stiff and glossy but not dry. Whisk in the vanilla. Place 4 to 6 large spoonfuls of meringue in the milk and simmer for 2 to 3 minutes, then turn the meringues and cook for another 2 to 3 minutes until firm to the touch. Using a slotted spoon, transfer the meringues to serving plates. Pour some crème anglaise around the floating island and garnish with some sugared cloudberries.

Here's an idea: If you don't have cloudberries on hand, try this with raspberries instead!

LIME TART WITH CHOCOLATE COFFEE GANACHE

Calamondin limes are very special and worth looking for, so ask for them. If you can't find them and don't have the time to fly to California and pick your own then I suggest you use tiny key limes or a combination of mandarin orange and lemon juice.

Serves 10 to 12

For the Chocolate Coffee Ganache
½ cup (125 mL) heavy cream
2 tbsp (30 mL) instant coffee granules
8 ounces (125 mL) finely chopped dark chocolate
1 baked sweet tart shell (see opposite page)

For the Calamondin Curd
5 large eggs
3 egg yolks
1 cup (250 mL) sugar
¾ cup (175 mL) calamondin juice
2 tbsp (30 mL) cold unsalted butter

To make the ganache, bring the cream and instant coffee to a boil in a small saucepan. Place the chocolate in a bowl and pour the cream over it. Let stand for 2 minutes. Stir with a wooden spoon until the chocolate is melted and the mixture is smooth. Spread the ganache evenly on the crust. Chill for at least 15 minutes.

While the crust is chilling, preheat your oven to 325°F (160°C). Meanwhile, make the curd. In the top of a double boiler, or in a large heatproof bowl set over a saucepan of simmering water, whisk together the eggs, egg yolks, sugar, and calamondin juice. Cook, stirring often, until translucent and thick enough to mound on a spoon, 15 to 20 minutes. Strain the curd through a fine sieve into bowl, then stir in the butter until melted.

Pour the curd into the tart shell, smoothing the top. Bake for about 12 minutes, until the filling sets. Let cool on a rack.

Cut the tart into slices and serve with sweet vanilla whipped cream.

1½ cups (375 mL) all-purpose flour
½ cup (125 mL) confectioner's sugar
¼ tsp (1 mL) salt
1 stick plus 1 tbsp (4½ ounces/125 mL) cold unsalted butter,
    cut into small pieces
1 large egg, lightly beaten

In a food processor, combine the flour, sugar, and salt; pulse to mix. Add the butter and process until the mixture resembles coarse meal. Add the egg; pulse until the dough starts to form clumps. Turn the dough out onto a work surface and knead the dough just to incorporate. Chill the dough, wrapped in plastic, for about 1 hour before rolling.

On a lightly floured surface, roll the dough into an 11-inch (28 cm) circle. Carefully fit it into a tart pan with a removable bottom. Pat some of the overhang back in around the edge to make the sides of the tart shell a bit thicker than the bottom. Trim off any remaining overhang. Refrigerate until firm, about 30 minutes.

Preheat your oven to 400°F (200°C). With a fork, prick the bottom at ½-inch (1 cm) intervals. Line with parchment paper and fill with pie weights or dried beans. Bake until the top of the rim starts to turn golden, 15 to 20 minutes. Remove weights and the parchment. Return to the oven and bake until golden, about 10 minutes. Cool on a rack.

SWEET PASTRY SHELL

Makes 1 9-inch (23 cm) round tart shell

ZUCCHINI OLIVE OIL CAKE

While working on the Lucero family's olive farm in Corning, California, I wanted to create a dessert that would make Dewey Lucero and his family proud. This family has been growing olives for three generations. This olive oil cake is incredibly moist and delicious, dressed with a sweet orange glaze and garnished with a salty-sweet olive brittle.

Serves 8 to 10

For the Walnut Olive Brittle
1 cup (250 mL) sugar
¼ cup (60 mL) water
½ cup (125 mL) finely chopped walnuts
2 tbsp (30 mL) finely chopped pitted black olives

For the Zucchini Olive Oil Cake
2 cups (500 mL) all-purpose flour
1 tsp (5 mL) kosher salt
1 tsp (5 mL) baking powder
½ tsp (2 mL) baking soda
2 tsp (10 mL) cinnamon
1 tsp (5 mL) ground ginger
½ tsp (2 mL) nutmeg

3 large eggs
1¾ cups (425 mL) sugar
1 cup (250 mL) extra-virgin olive oil
2 tsp (10 mL) vanilla extract
2½ cups (625 mL) grated zucchini
1 cup (250 mL) chopped walnuts
Sweet Vanilla Whipped Cream (page 216) for serving

For the Mandarin Orange Glaze
½ cup (125 mL) sugar
6 mandarin oranges, segmented and crushed
2 tbsp (30 mL) unsalted butter
1 tbsp (15 mL) heavy cream

To make the brittle, line a baking sheet with nonstick liner or with an oiled sheet of foil. In a deep, heavy saucepan over low heat, heat the sugar with the water. Stir slowly with a fork until sugar is melted and pale gold. Gently swirl the pan and stir in the walnuts and black olives, then immediately pour the mixture onto the baking sheet, tilting the sheet to spread the caramel as thinly as possible. Cool the brittle completely at room temperature. Break into small pieces with a spoon. This can be done ahead and kept in an airtight container.

To make the zucchini cake, preheat your oven to 350°F (180°C). Spray a Bundt cake pan with cooking spray, then dust with flour to coat it completely, tapping out the excess flour.

In a medium bowl, sift together the flour, salt, baking powder, baking soda, cinnamon, ginger, and nutmeg. In the bowl of an electric mixer fitted with the paddle attachment, beat the eggs, sugar, and olive oil on medium speed until light and fluffy, 3 to 4 minutes. Beat in the vanilla extract. Scrape down the sides of the bowl with a spatula, add the flour on low speed until combined, then beat on medium speed for 30 seconds. Stop the mixer and stir in the zucchini and the walnuts until they are completely incorporated. Pour the batter into the prepared pan, smoothing the top with a spatula. Bake for 45 to 50 minutes, until a tester inserted in the centre comes out clean and the cake has begun to pull away from the sides of the pan. Turn the cake out onto a rack and cool completely.

To make the glaze, in a small saucepan over medium-high heat, bring the sugar and ¼ cup (60 mL) of water to a boil. Cook, swirling the pan occasionally, until the sugar syrup is a medium golden brown. Add the mandarin orange juice. Whisk in the butter and heavy cream. Stir in the mandarin orange segments.

To serve, cut the cake into slices. Pour some of the glaze over the cake. Top with sweet vanilla whipped cream and walnut olive brittle.

STRAW-BERRY RHUBARB FOOL & SHORT-BREAD COOKIES

Irish moss is a totally natural seaweed that gives its thickening qualities to desserts and ice creams without any oceanic taste. I suggest you head to Prince Edward Island and pick some for yourself, or maybe just order it online. This is basically a strawberry-rhubarb fool served with the custard and some classic Scottish shortbread cookies.

Serves 8

For the Irish Moss Custard
3 large egg yolks
¼ cup (60 mL) sugar
1¼ cups (300 mL) milk
½ vanilla bean, split lengthwise
¼ cup (60 mL) Irish moss
1 tbsp (15 mL) Grand Marnier
1 tsp (5 mL) grated orange zest

For the Strawberry Rhubarb Sauce
2 cups (500 mL) rhubarb cut into
    1-inch (2.5 cm) pieces
¼ cup (60 mL) sugar
½ cup (125 mL) orange juice
1 tbsp (15 mL) grated orange zest
1 tbsp (15 mL) finely grated peeled
    ginger
2 cups (500 mL) strawberries, sliced

For the Shortbread Cookies
2 cups (500 mL) all-purpose flour
¾ tsp (4 mL) salt
1¼ cups (300 mL) unsalted butter,
    at room temperature
½ cup (125 mL) icing sugar
1 tsp (5 mL) vanilla extract

To make the custards, in a bowl, whisk together the egg yolks and sugar to combine. In a medium saucepan, bring the milk and vanilla bean to a boil over medium heat. Slowly pour the milk into the egg mixture, whisking constantly to prevent lumps. Remove the vanilla bean, scrape out the seeds, and add the seeds to the egg mixture. Return the egg mixture to the saucepan and add the Irish moss. Bring to a boil over medium heat, whisking constantly. Once it boils, whisk constantly for another 30 to 60 seconds as it thickens. Remove from heat and strain. Whisk in the Grand Marnier and orange zest. Pour into dessert cups and refrigerate until set, about 2 hours.

To make the sauce, in a saucepan combine the rhubarb, sugar, orange juice and zest, and ginger. Cook over medium heat until the rhubarb is slightly tender, 4 to 5 minutes. Stir in the strawberries and cook until they are softened, about 5 minutes. Remove from heat and let cool.

To make the shortbread cookies, in a bowl, whisk the flour with the salt. In the bowl of a mixer fitted with the paddle attachment, beat the butter until fluffy, 3 to 5 minutes. Add the icing sugar and continue to beat until pale and fluffy, occasionally scraping down the sides of the bowl, about 2 minutes more. Beat in the vanilla. Add flour mixture and mix on low speed, scraping sides if necessary, until the flour is incorporated and the dough sticks together. Divide the dough in half and shape each half into a disc. Wrap in plastic and chill until firm, about 1 hour.

Line a baking sheet with parchment paper. On a lightly floured surface, roll out 1 disc to ¼-inch (5 mm) thickness. Using a 2-inch (5 cm) cookie cutter, cut into rounds. Transfer to prepared baking sheet. Repeat with remaining dough. Refrigerate until firm, at least 30 minutes.

Meanwhile, preheat your oven to 325°F (160°C). Bake the cookies until firm and golden, 13 to 15 minutes. Cool completely on racks.

To serve, top the Irish moss custard with some of the strawberry rhubarb sauce. Serve with shortbread cookies.

PUMPKIN STICKY TOFFEE PUDDINGS

A fall favourite, warm and sweet, with the tart cranberries adding balance and an original spin on an old English favourite. I make this recipe just for the smell of it baking in the oven.

Makes 12 puddings

For the Pumpkin Sticky Toffee Puddings
2 cups (500 mL) all-purpose flour
2 tsp (10 mL) baking powder
¼ tsp (1 mL) baking soda
1 tsp (5 mL) cinnamon
¾ tsp (4 mL) ground ginger
⅛ tsp (0.5 mL) ground allspice
⅛ tsp (0.5 mL) ground cloves
½ tsp (2 mL) salt
½ cup (125 mL) unsalted butter, melted and cooled
¾ cup (175 mL) packed light brown sugar
¾ cup (175 mL) canned pumpkin purée
¼ cup (60 mL) buttermilk
2 large eggs
1 tsp (5 mL) vanilla extract
Sweet Vanilla Whipped Cream (page 216)
½ cup (125 mL) dried cranberries

For the Cranberry Caramel Sauce
1 cup (250 mL) sugar
3 tbsp (50 mL) heavy cream
3 tbsp (50 mL) unsalted butter
3 tbsp (50 mL) dried cranberries

To make the sticky toffee puddings, preheat your oven to 400°F (200°C).

Spray a nonstick muffin pan with cooking spray. In a large bowl, whisk together the flour, baking powder, baking soda, cinnamon, ginger, allspice, cloves, and salt. In a separate bowl, whisk together the butter, brown sugar, pumpkin purée, buttermilk, eggs, and vanilla. Add to dry ingredients and stir just until combined. Divide the batter among the muffin cups. Bake until a toothpick comes out clean, about 20 minutes. Cool in the pans for 5 minutes, then turn the muffins onto a cool rack.

Meanwhile, make the sauce. In a medium saucepan, cook the sugar over medium-low heat, stirring slowly with a fork until the sugar is melted and pale gold. Cook the caramel, gently swirling the pan, until deep golden. Remove from heat and carefully add the cream and butter. Return to heat and simmer, stirring, until the caramel is dissolved. Remove from heat and stir in the dried cranberries.

To serve, slice the muffins horizontally into 3. Pour the cranberry caramel sauce between each layer. Top puddings with a large spoon of sweet vanilla whipped cream and a sprinkle of dried cranberries.

4 apples
½ cup (125 mL) dark brown sugar
½ cup (125 mL) golden raisins
¼ cup (60 mL) dark rum
1 tsp (5 mL) grated lemon zest

½ tsp (2 mL) cinnamon
6 sheets phyllo pastry
½ cup (125 mL) unsalted butter, melted
2 tbsp (30 mL) icing sugar
Sweet Vanilla Whipped Cream (page 216)

RUM RAISIN APPLE STRUDEL

I made this strudel at a Knights of Columbus hall in Minnesota. The kitchen was humble so I decided to make a simplified strudel that could be assembled with a minimum of fuss. The end result is delicious and crackling with flaky phyllo. Slice, plate, and cover each portion almost completely in whipped cream. The more whipped cream the better!

Serves 6

Preheat your oven to 400°F (200°C). Peel and core the apples, then thinly slice them. In a large bowl, toss the apple slices with the brown sugar, raisins, rum, lemon zest, and cinnamon; set aside.

Place 1 sheet of phyllo pastry on a baking sheet. Cover remaining phyllo with a damp cloth. Brush the phyllo sheet with some melted butter. Layer the remaining sheets of phyllo on top, brushing each sheet with butter. About 2 inches (5 cm) from one long edge of pastry, spoon the apple mixture lengthwise along the pastry in a 3-inch (8 cm) wide strip, leaving a 2-inch (5 cm) border at each short end. Starting at the long edge nearest the filling, carefully fold the phyllo over the filling. Roll up the strudel jelly-roll style, folding in the edges as you roll. Roll up firmly but allow a little slack for expansion. Arrange the strudel in the middle of the baking sheet; brush it with butter. Bake until crisp and golden, 30 to 35 minutes. Transfer to a rack or serving platter and cool slightly.

Just before serving, dust the strudel with the icing sugar, cut into portions, and serve with sweet vanilla whipped cream.

CHEF LYNN'S BASICS

STOCKS & GRAVIES

CHICKEN STOCK

Makes 3 quarts (3 L)

4 lb (2 kg) chicken bones (wings, backs, and necks)
2 tbsp (30 mL) vegetable oil
4 carrots, quartered
3 onions, quartered
4 stalks celery, quartered

1 leek, cut into thirds, white and pale green parts only
4 cloves garlic
6 sprigs parsley
3 sprigs thyme
2 bay leaves
¼ tsp (1 mL) black peppercorns

Place all of the ingredients into a large pot. Fill the pot with cold water until it just covers the chicken bones. Over high heat, slowly bring the water to a boil. Reduce the temperature to a simmer. Using a ladle, skim off the foam as it appears at the top of your stock. Continue this until there is very little foam on top, about 1 hour. Continue to simmer the chicken stock until it develops a rich, chicken flavour, about 3 hours.

Remove the pot from heat. Pour the stock through a mesh strainer into a container. Fill your kitchen sink with ice and water. Cool the strained stock as quickly as possible. Cover and refrigerate for up to 1 week or freeze up to 3 months.

ROASTED CHICKEN STOCK

Makes 1 quart (1 L)

4 lb (2 kg) chicken bones, rinsed and cut into pieces
1 carrot, cut into 1-inch (2.5 cm) pieces
2 shallots, quartered lengthwise
1 stalk celery, cut into 1-inch (2.5 cm) pieces

1 cup (250 mL) white wine
2 sprigs thyme
4 sprigs parsley
5 peppercorns
3 quarts (3 L) chicken stock
Salt and pepper

Preheat your oven to 425°F (220°C). Roast the chicken bones until golden brown. Transfer bones to a stockpot. Add the carrot, shallots, and celery to the roasting pan. Return to the oven for another 8 minutes, until the vegetables are golden brown. Using a slotted spoon, transfer the vegetables to the stockpot. Set the roasting pan over two burners. Add the white wine and bring to a boil, scraping up any brown bits from the bottom of the pan. Boil until the liquid is reduced by half. Pour everything into the stockpot. Add the thyme, parsley, peppercorns, and chicken stock. Bring to a boil, then reduce heat and simmer. Using a ladle, skim off the foam as it appears at the top of your stock. Continue this until there is very little foam on top, about 1 hour. Continue to simmer stock until it has reduced by two-thirds, about 2 hours.

Remove the pot from heat. Pour the stock through a mesh strainer into a container. Fill your kitchen sink with ice and water. Cool the strained stock as quickly as possible. Cover and refrigerate for up to 1 week or freeze up to 3 months.

VEAL STOCK

Makes 4 quarts (4 L)

5 lb (2.5 kg) veal bones (knuckles and shins)
3 tbsp (50 mL) canola oil
2 leeks, cut into thirds, white and pale green parts only
3 onions, unpeeled, cut in half
4 stalks celery, cut into thirds
3 carrots, quartered
1 head garlic, cut in half crosswise
2 tbsp (30 mL) tomato paste
1 cup (250 mL) water
½ bunch parsley
5 sprigs thyme
3 bay leaves
2 tsp (10 mL) black peppercorns
½ split chopped calf's foot

Preheat your oven to 425°F (220°C). Spread the veal bones in a large roasting pan. Drizzle with oil and turn to coat. Roast until dark golden brown, about 1 hour, turning them from time to time with a slotted spoon. Transfer the bones to a large stockpot and set aside. Spread the leeks, onions, celery, carrots, and garlic in the roasting pan and return to the oven for about 20 minutes. Using a wooden spoon, stir the vegetables and scrape any browned bits off the bottom of the pan. Add the tomato paste and roast for another 5 minutes. Transfer the vegetables to the stockpot. Set the roasting pan over two burners. Add the water and bring to a boil, scraping up any browned bits from the bottom of the roasting pan. Boil until liquid is reduced by half. Pour everything into the stockpot. Add enough water to cover the bones and vegetables by 2 inches (5 cm). Bring to a boil, then reduce heat to a bare simmer. Add the parsley, thyme, bay leaves, peppercorns, and calf's foot, and very gently simmer for 8 hours. Skim any fat or foam that rises to the top.

Strain the stock through a fine-mesh strainer into storing containers. Cool in ice water in the sink, stirring often to cool the stock as quickly as possible. Cover and refrigerate for up to 1 week or freeze up to 3 months.

FISH STOCK

Makes 2 quarts (2 L)

2 tbsp (30 mL) butter
1 stalk celery, cut into 1-inch (2.5 cm) pieces
1 onion, quartered
1 leek, thinly sliced, white only
½ fennel bulb, thinly sliced
10 white peppercorns
6 fennel seeds

1 bay leaf
2 sprigs thyme
Kosher salt
1 cup (250 mL) white wine
2 lb (1 kg) white fish bones, rinsed and chopped
Stems from ¼ bunch chervil
Stems from ¼ bunch parsley

Heat the butter in a large stockpot over medium-high heat. Add the celery, onion, leek, fennel, peppercorns, fennel seeds, bay leaf, thyme, and salt to taste. Cook, stirring, for 6 minutes or until the vegetables are soft but not coloured. Add the white wine and cook until it has reduced by half. Add the fish bones and enough cold water to just cover the bones. Bring to a boil, then reduce heat and simmer for 20 minutes, frequently skimming any foam that rises to the top. Add the chervil and parsley stems and cook for another 10 minutes.

Strain the stock through a fine-mesh strainer into storing containers. Cool in ice water in the sink, stirring often to cool the stock as quickly as possible. Cover and refrigerate for up to 4 days or freeze up to 3 months.

VEGETABLE STOCK

Makes 2 quarts (2 L)

2 leeks, whites only, thinly sliced
6 carrots, cut in 1-inch (2 cm) rounds
3 celery stalks, thinly sliced
3 onions, thinly sliced
Stems from ¼ bunch tarragon
Stems from ¼ bunch basil

Stems from ¼ bunch chervil
1 star anise
5 white peppercorns
5 fennel seeds
1 cup (250 mL) white wine
½ lemon, sliced

Place the leeks, carrots, celery, and onions in a large pot and add enough water to cover. Bring to a boil, reduce heat, and simmer for 10 minutes. Add the tarragon, basil, and chervil stems, the star anise, peppercorns, and fennel seeds; simmer for another 4 minutes. Remove from heat and stir in the white wine and lemon slices.

Strain the stock through a fine-mesh strainer into storing containers. Cool in ice water in the sink, stirring often to cool the stock as quickly as possible. Cover and refrigerate for up to 1 week or freeze up to 3 months.

QUICK TURKEY GRAVY

Makes 4 cups (1 L)

4 turkey wings
1 medium onion, peeled and diced
½ cup (125 mL) cup water
5 cups (1.25 L) chicken broth, divided
2 carrots, cut into ½-inch (1 cm) pieces
2 stalks of celery, cut into 1-inch
    (2.5 cm) pieces

2 sprigs of thyme
1 bay leaf
¼ cup (60 mL) all-purpose flour
2 tbsp (30 mL) unsalted butter
Salt and pepper

Preheat your oven to 400°F (200°C). Arrange the turkey wings in a large roasting pan. Scatter the onions over the wings and roast in the oven for 1 hour or until wings are browned.

Place browned wings and onions in a large stockpot. Add the water to the roasting pan and stir, scraping up any brown bits on the bottom of the pan. Pour the water from the pan into the stockpot. Stir in 4 cups of broth, carrot, celery, thyme, and bay leaf. Bring to a boil. Reduce heat to medium-low and simmer uncovered for 1½ hours.

Remove wings from the pot and strain contents of stockpot through a large strainer into a medium saucepan. Press on the vegetables to extract any remaining liquid. Discard the vegetables and skim the fat off the liquid. Bring the contents of the pot to a gentle boil.

In a medium bowl, whisk flour into the remaining 1 cup chicken broth until smooth. Gradually whisk the flour mixture into the simmering turkey broth; simmer 3 to 4 minutes or until the gravy has thickened. Stir in the butter and pepper. Serve immediately or pour into containers and refrigerate or freeze.

MAYONNAISES & OTHER SAUCES

MAYONNAISE
Makes 1 cup (250 mL)

2 large egg yolks
1 tbsp (15 mL) Dijon mustard
1 tbsp (15 mL) white wine vinegar

1 tbsp (15 mL) lemon juice
1 cup (250 mL) canola oil
Salt and pepper

In a large bowl, whisk together the egg yolks, mustard, vinegar, and lemon juice until thoroughly combined. Whisk in the oil in a slow, steady stream until the mayonnaise is thickened and emulsified. Season with salt and pepper.

CAJUN MAYONNAISE
Makes ½ cup (125 mL)

½ cup (125 mL) mayonnaise
1 green onion, thinly sliced

Juice of 1 lemon
1 tsp (5 mL) Cajun Seasoning (page 259)

In a bowl, stir together mayonnaise, onion, lemon juice, and Cajun seasoning. Cover and refrigerate until ready to use.

BASIL MAYONNAISE
Makes 1½ cups (375 mL)

2 cups (500 mL) loosely packed
    basil leaves
1 cup (250 mL) mayonnaise

2 tbsp (30 mL) lemon juice
1 tbsp (15 mL) Dijon mustard
Salt and pepper

In a food processor, pulse the basil, mayonnaise, lemon juice, and mustard until smooth. Season with salt and pepper. Cover and refrigerate until ready to use.

AÏOLI
Makes 1 cup (250 mL)

2 large egg yolks
1 tsp (5 mL) Dijon mustard
2 cloves garlic, grated

2 tbsp (30 mL) lemon juice
1 cup (250 mL) canola oil
Salt and pepper

In a medium bowl, whisk together the egg yolks, mustard, garlic, and lemon juice. Whisk in the oil in a slow, steady stream until the aïoli is thickened and emulsified. Season with salt and pepper.

AVOCADO AÏOLI
Makes 3 cups (750 mL)

3 avocados
½ cup (125 mL) sour cream
3 tbsp (50 mL) chopped basil
2 tbsp (30 mL) minced garlic
2 tbsp (30 mL) lemon juice

2 tbsp (30 mL) lime juice
1 jalapeño pepper, seeded and minced
1 bunch green onions, thinly sliced
Salt and pepper

Scoop the avocado flesh into a medium bowl and coarsely mash with a fork. Fold in the sour cream, basil, garlic, lemon juice, lime juice, jalapeño, and green onions. Season with salt and pepper and serve immediately.

SAFFRON AÏOLI
Makes 1 cup (250 mL)

1 large pinch saffron threads
2 large egg yolks
1 tsp (5 mL) Dijon mustard
2 cloves garlic, grated

2 tbsp (30 mL) lemon juice
1 cup (250 mL) olive oil
Salt and pepper

In small saucepan, bring the saffron threads and 1 tbsp (15 mL) water to a boil. Set aside to cool.

In a medium bowl, whisk together the egg yolks, mustard, garlic, and lemon juice. Whisk in the oil in a slow, steady stream until the aïoli is thickened and emulsified. Stir in the saffron and season with salt and pepper.

HORSE-RADISH AÏOLI
Makes ½ cup (125 mL)

½ cup (125 mL) mayonnaise
2 tbsp (30 mL) prepared horseradish

1 tbsp (15 mL) lemon juice
Salt and pepper to taste

In a small bowl, stir together all the ingredients.

CILANTRO FINGER LIME AÏOLI

Makes 1 cup (250 mL)

4 large egg yolks
Zest and juice of 2 limes
1 tsp (5 mL) Dijon mustard
2 cloves garlic, minced
1 bunch cilantro, chopped
1 cup (250 mL) olive oil
2 to 4 whole finger limes
Salt and pepper

In a food processor, combine the egg yolks, lime zest and juice, mustard, garlic, and cilantro; process until puréed. With the machine running, add the oil in a steady stream until incorporated and emulsified. Transfer the aïoli to a bowl. Cut the finger limes in half and squeeze the pulp into the aïoli. Stir well and season with salt and pepper.

LEMON RÉMOULADE

Makes 1½ cups (375 mL)

1 cup (250 mL) mayonnaise (page 250)
Juice and zest of 2 lemons
2 tbsp (30 mL) minced cornichons
2 tbsp (30 mL) minced capers
2 tbsp (30 mL) chopped parsley
2 tbsp (30 mL) chopped chives
Salt and pepper to taste

Whisk all the ingredients together in a small bowl. Refrigerate until ready to use.

LEMON MUSTARD RÉMOULADE

Makes 1½ cups (375 mL)

To the above recipe, add 2 tbsp (30 mL) grainy mustard.

GRIBICHE SAUCE

Makes 1 cup (250 mL)

¼ cup (60 mL) mayonnaise (page 250)
¼ cup (60 mL) sour cream
Juice of 2 lemons
4 hard-boiled eggs, finely chopped
2 tbsp (30 mL) finely chopped capers
2 tbsp (30 mL) finely chopped cornichons
2 tbsp (30 mL) finely chopped parsley
1 tbsp (15 mL) finely chopped chervil
1 tbsp (15 mL) finely chopped tarragon
1 tbsp (15 mL) finely chopped shallot
Salt and pepper

In a small bowl, whisk together the mayonnaise, sour cream, and lemon juice. Stir in the eggs, capers, cornichons, parsley, chervil, tarragon, and shallot. Season sauce to taste with salt and pepper.

BASIL PESTO

Makes 2 cups (500 mL)

3 cups (750 mL) loosely packed basil
    leaves
¼ cup (60 mL) grated Parmesan cheese
2 tbsp (30 mL) pine nuts, toasted

2 cloves garlic
1 cup (250 mL) extra-virgin olive oil
Salt and pepper

In a food processor, combine the basil, Parmesan, pine nuts, garlic, and ¼ cup (60 mL) of the olive oil. Process until smooth, scraping down the sides of the bowl. With the machine running, add the remaining olive oil in a slow, steady stream until the pesto has thickened. Season with salt and pepper.

HERB PESTO

Makes 2 cups (500 mL)

1½ cups (375 mL) basil leaves
¼ cup (60 mL) flat-leaf parsley leaves
¼ cup (60 mL) green onions, coarsely
    chopped
½ cup (125 mL) pine nuts, toasted

½ cup (125 mL) grated Parmesan cheese
2 cloves garlic
⅓ cup (75 mL) extra-virgin olive oil
Salt and pepper

In a food processor, combine the basil, parsley, green onions, pine nuts, Parmesan, and garlic. Process until the herbs are finely chopped. Add the oil and process to a coarse purée. Season with salt and pepper.

BEURRE BLANC

Makes ⅔ cup (150 mL)

¼ cup (60 mL) good white wine
¼ cup (60 mL) white wine vinegar
2 shallots, finely chopped
2 tbsp (30 mL) heavy cream

½ cup (125 mL) cold unsalted butter,
    cut into cubes
2 tsp (10 mL) lemon juice
Salt and pepper

Put the wine, vinegar, and shallots in a small saucepan. Simmer over medium-high heat until the liquid is reduced by half, about 6 minutes. Whisk in the cream and return to a simmer. Reduce heat to low and whisk in the butter, a few pieces at a time, until completely emulsified. Season with lemon juice, salt, and pepper. Strain the sauce through a fine sieve.

CLARIFIED BUTTER

Makes 1½ cups (375 mL)

1 lb (500 g) unsalted butter

In a small saucepan over very low heat, melt the butter and bring it slowly to a boil. Skim off the froth from the surface. Carefully pour the liquid butter into a bowl, taking care not to include any of the milky sediment from the bottom of the pot. The clarified butter will keep in the refrigerator for several weeks.

HOLLANDAISE SAUCE

Makes 1½ cups (375 mL)

5 egg yolks
1 cup (250 mL) clarified butter, warm

2 tbsp (30 mL) lemon juice
Salt and pepper

Put the egg yolks in a bowl and set the bowl over a pot half full of simmering water. Whisk the yolks for 2 to 3 minutes until they thicken slightly. Make sure to move the bowl on and off the heat as necessary to avoid cooking the eggs. Remove the bowl from the heat and begin adding the clarified butter slowly at first, a few drops at a time, while whisking constantly. If you add it too quickly, the emulsion will break. Whisk in the lemon juice, season with salt and pepper, and serve immediately.

MOUSSELINE SAUCE

Makes 2 cups (500 mL)

1½ cups (375 mL) freshly made
    Hollandaise Sauce
2 tbsp (30 mL) lemon juice

½ cup (125 mL) heavy cream, whipped
Salt and black pepper
Cayenne pepper

In a bowl, whisk together the hollandaise sauce and lemon juice, then fold in the cream. Season with salt, black pepper, and cayenne to taste. Serve immediately.

2 tbsp (30 mL) olive oil
1 onion, finely chopped
3 cloves garlic, finely chopped
⅛ tsp (0.5 mL) chili flakes
1 tbsp (15 mL) tomato paste

1 tsp (5 mL) sugar
1 can (28 oz/796 mL) chopped tomatoes
Salt and pepper
2 tbsp (30 mL) chopped parsley
2 tbsp (30 mL) chopped basil

TOMATO SAUCE

Makes 4 cups (1 L)

In a large pot, heat the oil over medium heat. Add the onions, garlic, and chili flakes. Cook until the onions are golden brown, about 6 minutes. Stir in the tomato paste and sugar; cook for an additional 2 minutes. Add the tomatoes and their juices. Season with salt and pepper. Bring to a boil, stirring, then reduce heat and simmer for 30 minutes, until the sauce thickens. Remove from heat and stir in the parsley and basil.

2 tbsp (30 mL) canola oil
2 onions, finely chopped
4 cloves garlic, grated
2 cups (500 mL) crushed tomatoes
1 cup (250 mL) ketchup
2 tbsp (30 mL) tomato paste

1 canned chipotle chili in adobo sauce, minced
2 tbsp (30 mL) cider vinegar
2 tbsp (30 mL) Dijon mustard
¼ cup (60 mL) maple syrup
Salt and black pepper

BARBECUE SAUCE

Makes 4 cups (1 L)

In a medium saucepan, heat the oil over medium heat. Add the onions and garlic. Cook, stirring, until the onions are soft and translucent, about 5 minutes. Stir in the tomatoes, ketchup, tomato paste, chipotle, cider vinegar, mustard, and maple syrup. Reduce heat to medium-low and simmer, stirring occasionally, until reduced by one-quarter, about 45 minutes. Working in batches, purée sauce in a blender. Season with salt and pepper. The sauce keeps, covered and refrigerated, for up to 2 weeks.

1 cup (250 mL) ketchup
2 tbsp (30 mL) prepared horseradish
2 tbsp (30 mL) lemon juice

1 tsp (5 mL) Worcestershire sauce
Dash hot pepper sauce
Salt and pepper

COCKTAIL SAUCE

Makes 1¼ cups (300 mL)

In a small bowl, stir together all the ingredients until well combined.

VINAIGRETTES

BROWN DERBY VINAIGRETTE

Makes 2 cups (500 mL)

¼ cup (60 mL) red wine vinegar
2 tsp (10 mL) balsamic vinegar
2 tbsp (30 mL) honey
1 tbsp (15 mL) Worcestershire sauce

¼ tsp (1 mL) kosher salt
Juice of 1 lemon
2 tbsp (30 mL) Dijon mustard
1⅓ cups (325 mL) canola oil

In a medium bowl, whisk together the red wine vinegar, balsamic vinegar, honey, Worcestershire sauce, salt, and lemon juice until the salt dissolves. Whisk in the mustard. Whisking constantly, slowly drizzle in the oil until emulsified. Transfer to a container and store in the refrigerator.

LEMON HERB VINAIGRETTE

Makes 2 cups (500 mL)

¼ cup (60 mL) lemon juice
¼ cup (60 mL) white wine vinegar
1 tsp (5 mL) Dijon mustard
2 tbsp (30 mL) minced shallots
½ tsp (2 mL) salt

1½ cups (375 mL) canola oil
1 tsp (5 mL) finely chopped parsley
1 tsp (5 mL) finely chopped chervil
1 tsp (5 mL) finely chopped chives

In a medium bowl, whisk together the lemon juice, vinegar, mustard, shallots, and salt. Add the oil in a slow stream, whisking until emulsified. Add the parsley, chervil, and chives, and stir until fully incorporated.

SHERRY SHALLOT VINAIGRETTE

Makes 2 cups (500 mL)

½ cup (125 mL) sherry vinegar
2 tbsp (30 mL) minced shallots

1 cup (250 mL) canola oil
½ cup (125 mL) olive oil

Whisk all the ingredients together in a small bowl until emulsified. Season with salt and pepper.

¼ cup (60 mL) oil-packed sun-dried
    tomatoes, drained and chopped
2 tbsp (30 mL) balsamic vinegar
2 tbsp (30 mL) red wine vinegar
2 tbsp (30 mL) minced shallots

1 clove garlic, minced
½ cup (125 mL) olive oil
1 tbsp (15 mL) chopped basil
Salt and pepper

BASIL SUN-DRIED TOMATO VINAIGRETTE

Makes 1 cup (250 mL)

In a small bowl, whisk together the tomatoes, balsamic vinegar, wine vinegar, shallots, and garlic. Add the oil in a stream, whisking constantly until the vinaigrette is emulsified. Stir in the basil. Season with salt and pepper.

¼ cup (60 mL) cloudberries
Zest and juice of 2 oranges
3 tbsp (50 mL) honey
2 tbsp (30 mL) white balsamic vinegar

1 clove garlic, peeled
Salt and pepper
¾ cup (175 mL) extra-virgin olive oil

BALSAMIC CLOUDBERRY VINAIGRETTE

Makes 1 cup (250 mL)

In a blender, combine the cloudberries, orange zest and juice, honey, vinegar, garlic, and salt and pepper. Blend until smooth. With the blender running, add the oil in a steady stream until combined. Strain through a sieve. Transfer to a container and store in the refrigerator.

¼ cup (60 mL) pomegranate molasses
3 tbsp (50 mL) honey
2 tbsp (30 mL) red wine vinegar
Zest and juice of 1 orange
1 tbsp (15 mL) finely chopped shallots

1 tsp (5 mL) minced garlic
1 tsp (5 mL) Dijon mustard
¾ cup (175 mL) pecan oil
3 tbsp (50 mL) finely chopped parsley
Salt and pepper

PECAN POMEGRANATE VINAIGRETTE

Makes 1 cup (250 mL)

In a small bowl, combine the pomegranate molasses, honey, vinegar, orange zest and juice, shallots, garlic, and mustard; stir together well. Add the oil in a slow stream, whisking until emulsified. Whisk in the parsley. Season with salt and pepper.

2 shallots, finely diced
Zest and juice of 2 oranges
Zest and juice of 1 lemon

1 tsp (5 mL) Dijon mustard
¾ cup (175 mL) olive oil
Salt and pepper

CITRUS VINAIGRETTE

Makes 1 cup (250 mL)

In a small bowl, stir together the shallots, orange and lemon zests and juices, and mustard. Whisk in the oil in a steady stream until emulsified. Season with salt and pepper.

SPICE RUBS & MARINADES

MY OLD BAY SEASONING
Makes 3 tbsp (50 mL)

1 tbsp (15 mL) celery salt
1 tsp (5 mL) ground celery seeds
1 tsp (5 mL) dry mustard
1 tsp (5 mL) ground black pepper
1 tsp (5 mL) sweet paprika
1 tsp (5 mL) smoked paprika

½ tsp (2 mL) ground cloves
½ tsp (2 mL) ground ginger
⅛ tsp (0.5 mL) cayenne pepper
⅛ tsp (0.5 mL) ground mace
⅛ tsp (0.5 mL) ground cardamom
⅛ tsp (0.5 mL) ground allspice

Combine all the ingredients and mix thoroughly. Store in an airtight container in a cool place. Use with seafood or chicken.

CAJUN SEASONING
Makes ⅔ cup (150 mL)

⅓ cup (75 mL) smoked paprika
1 tbsp (15 mL) kosher salt
2 tsp (10 mL) onion powder
2 tsp (10 mL) garlic powder
2 tsp (10 mL) dried oregano

2 tsp (10 mL) dried basil
1 tsp (5 mL) dried thyme
1 tsp (5 mL) ground black pepper
1 tsp (5 mL) cayenne pepper

Combine all the ingredients and mix thoroughly. Store in an airtight container.

COWBOY STEAK RUB
Makes ½ cup (125 mL)

2 tbsp (30 mL) chopped thyme
1 tbsp (15 mL) kosher salt
1 tbsp (15 mL) freshly ground black
    pepper

1 tsp (5 mL) chili powder
1 tsp (5 mL) cayenne pepper

Combine all the ingredients and mix thoroughly. Store in an airtight container.

PIRI-PIRI SPICE RUB

Makes ¼ cup (60 mL)

1½ tsp (7 mL) smoked paprika
1 tsp (5 mL) dried oregano
1 tsp (5 mL) coarsely ground coriander
1 tsp (5 mL) coarsely ground black
  pepper
1 tsp (5 mL) ground ginger
1 tsp (5 mL) ground cardamom
1 tsp (5 mL) garlic powder
½ tsp (2 mL) salt
½ tsp (2 mL) ground piri-piri pepper

Combine all the ingredients and mix thoroughly. Store in an airtight container.

HARISSA PASTE

Makes 1 cup (250 mL)

¼ cup (60 mL) olive oil
2 tbsp (30 mL) ancho chili powder
2 tbsp (30 mL) tomato paste
5 cloves garlic, minced
2 tsp (10 mL) ground coriander
1 tsp (5 mL) ground caraway
1 tsp (5 mL) ground cumin
1 tsp (5 mL) sea salt
½ tsp (2 mL) cayenne pepper
A few drops of lemon juice

In a mini food processor, combine the oil, chili powder, tomato paste, garlic, coriander, caraway, cumin, salt, and cayenne. Process until smooth. Add a few drops of lemon juice. Can be stored in the refrigerator for up to a month.

PICKLED KOHLRABI

Makes 2 1-pint (500 mL) mason jars

2 cups (500 mL) distilled white vinegar
2 cups (500 mL) water
¾ cup (175 mL) sugar
⅓ cup (75 mL) kosher salt
1 tsp (5 mL) yellow mustard seeds
½ tsp (2 mL) chili flakes
1 red onion, sliced
2 to 3 kohlrabi, peeled and thinly sliced

In a medium saucepan, combine the vinegar, water, sugar, salt, mustard seeds, and chili flakes. Bring to a boil. Place the onions and kohlrabi in another saucepan. Strain the pickling liquid over the vegetables. Bring to a boil, then remove from heat. Let cool to room temperature. Pour into mason jars and refrigerate.

THANKS

As an apprentice in the world of writing cookbooks, I must admit I had no idea what I was in for! I have learnt so much and have grown so much as a chef in the process. This has been an amazing experience and I am very grateful to have had all of the immense support and unconditional generosity of many friends, colleagues and artists who have helped me write this book.

Thanks to the team at Penguin Group (Canada). Special thanks go to my editor, Andrea Magyar, for all of her guidance, expertise and enthusiasm for this book, talented art director, Mary Opper, who made this book look absolutely incredible, managing editor Mary Ann Blair and copy editor Shaun Oakey.

Thanks to Kathleen Finlay, for your stunning photography and commitment to get the best shot every time. You are so talented and I am very grateful to have worked with you on this book.

Thanks to Sasha Seymour, for making the food look so beautiful and delicious with the great style and magic that you possess.

Thanks to Lora Kirk for your culinary expertise, professionalism and hours of recipe writing, testing and food styling. What fun it was! I could not have done this without you.

Thanks to Eliza Clark and Ivy Knight, for your beautiful words and for capturing the extraordinary places I visited and the amazing people I met.

Thanks to Kuba Psuty, you are a talented artist and friend. Thank you for the amazing gift of your beautiful photographs, which I am so thrilled to have included in this book for everyone else to enjoy.

Thanks to Rachel Low, for the opportunity to work together and see a project go from an idea to reality. *Pitchin' In* has been one of the most rewarding and incredible chapters in my life and I am very proud of it.

even more thanks ☞

Thanks to Jamie Brown and Lynne Skromeda at Frantic Films for all of your assistance in making this book happen.

Thanks to my entire *Pitchin' In* family, past and present, who I've shared so many adventures with on the road and behind the scenes making our show so great, memorable and fun: Meagan McAteer, Kristoff Rochon, Mikey Kulinski, Kuba Psuty, Brett Shama, Sarah Peddie, Mark Toller, Adam Hurlburt, Ben Sulzenko, Stefanie Haist, Donna Luke, Ivy Knight, Karina Baylon, Cheryl Zalameda, Leslie Lucas, Eliza Clark, Nikki Chow, John McMullan, James MacDonald, David Yohans, Steve Perrett, Julie Martin, Mic Forsey, Jacqueline Tam, Jeff Krebs, Michael Beard, Stephanie Fast, Rania Eid, Todd Buttenham, Colin Cooper, Marlen Da Silva, Rita Su, Sergio Alvarado, Jennifer Low, Erin Sharp, and Tim Trojian.

Thanks to Daniel Gelfant for always being there for me. Thank you for your vision and all that you give to our show (including your recipe suggestions!). I love that you are a chef at heart and that you love food and cooking as much as I do.

Thanks to Food Network Canada, especially Leslie Merklinger, Emily Morgan, Jaclyn Atwood, and Kathy Cross for the support that you have always given me.

Thanks to my amazingly talented and passionate staff at Ruby Watchco, who inspire me each and everyday.

Thank you, Cherie and Joey, for all of your love and support.

Thanks to all of the passionate farmers and fishermen I met, who have inspired me to cook with all of my heart: Andrew and Jennifer Thompson, Eric Thomas, Billie Dischler, Jamie Conques, Frank Gillis, Stanton Seamone, Lavena Crocker, Danny Williamson, Deborah and George Amrein-Boyes, Andrew and Jenn Harrison, Captain Corey Rock, Kevin McLarren, Stephen Ashley, Rob Rudel, Lee Grey, Dewey Lucero and family, Mary Mitchell, Teena and Mike Borek, Dave and Flo Minar, Doug Lau, Nancy and Bill Wilkie, Ron Joyce, Sebnem Ucer, Stephen Stewart, Ralph Bernard, Goldie Gillis, Lutz Zilliken, Kay Dinh, Gary Sweetnam and Cynthia Austin, Jim Iamurri, Vic MacKenzie, Cid da Silva, Gerry and Doris Hussey, Cam Beard, Rosemary Wotske, Fred and Ingrid de Martines, Joe Terzoli, Vince Terzoli, Ercole Terzoli, Vernon and Beth Hiebert, Robert Faircloth, Tim Montz, Jake Montz, Tracy Cornwell, and Lisle and Mary Lou Babcock.

My most heartfelt thanks to Lora, for your love, support, passion, talent, laughter, commitment, love of food and wine, and respect for those who give us beautiful ingredients to cook with. We have created a beautiful book together.

INDEX